MURDER & MAYHEM
ON CHICAGO'S
WEST SIDE

MURDER & MAYHEM
ON CHICAGO'S
WEST SIDE

TROY TAYLOR

Charleston   London

THE
History
PRESS

Published by The History Press
Charleston, SC 29403
www.historypress.net

Copyright © 2009 by Troy Taylor
All rights reserved

First published 2009

Manufactured in the United States

ISBN 978.1.59629.693.0

Library of Congress Cataloging-in-Publication Data

Taylor, Troy.
Murder & mayhem on Chicago's West Side / Troy Taylor.
p. cm.
Includes bibliographical references.
ISBN 978-1-59629-693-0
1. Murder--Illinois--Chicago--History. 2. Crime--Illinois--Chicago--History. I. Title.
II. Title: Murder and mayhem on Chicago's West Side.
HV6534.C4T3935 2009
364.152'30977311--dc22
2009015725

CONTENTS

ACKNOWLEDGEMENTS

I would like to thank Jim Gracyzk for his keen interest in Chicago history and crime and for his continuing support on various projects. Again, thanks to the many writers and chroniclers of crime in the Windy City, especially Herbert Asbury, Jay Robert Nash and Richard Lindberg, and to the kind keepers of libraries, history rooms and archives who always went out of their way to help. Thanks also to Jonathan Simcosky at The History Press and my wife, Haven, for putting up with a lot of strange interests and for her patience during numerous side trips to crime scenes and murder sites.

INTRODUCTION

C hicago's West Side was always a desperate place. It was to this part of the city that refugees fled, seeking escape from not only the urban sprawl but also the memories of the lands where they once lived. The history of the West Side is a history of ordinary people—immigrants, the working class and the poor and downtrodden—who came looking for a better life in the crowded tenements west of Halsted Street.

During the years of growth that occurred before and just after the Civil War, many first- and second-generation Irish, Germans, Scandinavians and Americans from the mid-South settled on the West Side. In those days, this area was still a fashionable neighborhood and a part of Chicago's West Division, but that was soon to change. As the great industrial boom began on the West Side, foundries, rolling mills and smokestacks drove out the original residents, and the once fine homes were replaced by one of the poorest working-class neighborhoods in the city. Then, in a hay barn on the near West Side, the devastation that became known as the Great Chicago Fire broke out in 1871.

According to legend, the fire was started by a cow that belonged to an Irishwoman named Catherine O'Leary. She ran a neighborhood milk business from the barn behind her home. She carelessly left a kerosene lantern in the barn after the evening milking, and a cow kicked it over and ignited the hay on the floor. Whether fact or fancy, the legend of Mrs. O'Leary's cow became an often-told tale in Chicago and eventually spread all over the world. However the fire started, on Sunday evening, October 8, 1871, Chicago became a city in flames.

The Great Chicago Fire began on October 8, 1871, first devastating the West Side of the city. Many lives were lost during the blaze, which turned Chicago into a smoldering ruin. *Courtesy of the Library of Congress.*

The Patrick O'Leary home, a small frame dwelling at 137 De Koven Street, was a lively place that night. O'Leary, his wife and their five children were already in bed, but the two front rooms of the house were rented to Patrick McLaughlin, a fiddler who, with his family and friends, was entertaining his wife's cousin, recently arrived from Ireland. The rooms were filled with music and drinking, and at some point, a few of the young men who were present went out to get another half gallon of beer—or so Mrs. McLaughlin would later swear.

Gossips in the neighborhood told a different story. They claimed that at some point in the evening, some of the McLaughlin clan decided to prepare an oyster stew for their party, and a couple of the young men were sent to get some milk from the cow that the O'Learys stabled in a barn at the rear of the house. A broken lamp found among the ashes of the stable a few days later gave rise to the legend that the cow, or a careless milker, had started the fire that destroyed Chicago.

No matter what the cause—and no one had time to hunt for clues or blame anyone on the night of October 8—the Great Chicago Fire broke out near the O'Leary barn on De Koven Street on the West Side. The home and

The O'Leary Cottage at 137 De Koven Street on Chicago's West Side. The fire began in the O'Learys' barn. Legend has it that a cow kicked over a lantern and this ignited the blaze, but it was more likely caused by careless revelers who broke into the barn looking for free milk. *Courtesy of the Chicago Historical Society.*

barn were located in the West Division neighborhood, an area of the city that was west of the south branch of the river. Conditions were perfect for a fire. The summer had been dry, and less than three inches of rain had fallen between July and October.

By ten o'clock that evening, the fire had spread from the O'Learys' across the West Side in two swaths so wide that all of the engines in town were clanging on the streets, and the courthouse bell, in the downtown section, pealed incessantly. Many things conspired to give the flames such headway in such a short amount of time. The watchman on the city hall tower had misjudged the blaze's location and called for a fire company that was located a mile and a half out of the way, causing a terrible delay. In addition, a strong, dry wind from the southwest was blowing. Furthermore, most of Chicago's fire companies had been exhausted by a fire on the West Side the day before and had celebrated the defeat of the blaze by getting drunk. The firemen had been working almost day and night all summer, battling one conflagration after another, and they needed to relax. The residents of "the city of shams and shingles" had believed that it would never burn. Fires might damage small neighborhoods but not the great city.

Within half an hour, all of Chicago was on the streets, running for the river. Most could not believe what they were seeing—a wall of flames, miles wide and hundreds of feet high, devoured the West Side and was carried on the wind toward the very heart of the city. By 10:30 p.m., it was officially out of control, and soon the mills and factories along the river were on fire. Buildings, even across the river, were hit by fiery missiles from the main blaze and began to burn. Owners of downtown buildings began throwing water on roofs and walls as the air filled with sparks and cinders, a sight contemporary accounts described as resembling red rain.

Even then, the crowds were sure that the flames would die out when they struck the blackened, four-block area that had burned during the previous night's fire. But with the force of hundreds of burning homes and buildings behind it, the blaze passed over the burned-out path, attacked the grain elevators along the river and fell upon Union Station.

From the West Side, a mob poured into the downtown section, jamming the bridges and flooding the streets. It was believed that the river would stop the fire in its path, but a blazing board that was carried on the wind settled on the roof of a tenement building at Adams and Franklin Streets, one-third of a mile from any burning building. The fire hungrily jumped the river and began pushing toward the center of the city. Fire engines, frantic to save the more valuable property of the business district, pushed back over the bridges from the West Side.

Among the first downtown buildings to be engulfed was the new Parmalee Omnibus & Stage Company at the southeast corner of Jackson and Franklin Streets. A flying brand also struck the South Side Gas Works, and soon this structure burst into flames, creating a new and larger center for the fire. At this point, even the grease- and oil-covered river caught fire, and the surface of the water shimmered with heat and flames.

In moments, the fire spread to the banks and office buildings along LaSalle Street. Soon, more than a dozen different locations were burning at once. The fire swept through Wells, Market and Franklin Streets, igniting more than five hundred different buildings. One by one, these great structures fell. The Tribune building, long vaunted as "fireproof," was turned into a

The ruins of the Chicago Courthouse after the fire. A bell tolled for hours, alerting people to danger, before the building was engulfed in flames. It was said that when the building collapsed, a roaring sound could be heard more than a mile away. *Courtesy of the Chicago Historical Society.*

smoking ruin, as was Marshall Field's grand department store and hundreds of other businesses.

In the early morning hours of Monday, the fire reached the courthouse, which stood in a block surrounded by LaSalle, Clark, Randolph and Washington Streets. A burning timber landed on the building's wooden cupola and soon turned into a fire that blazed out of control. The building was evacuated. The prisoners, who had begun to scream and shake the bars of their cells as smoke filled the air, were released. Most of them were allowed to simply go free, but the most dangerous of them were shackled and taken away under guard. Just after 2:00 a.m., the bell of the courthouse tolled for the last time before crashing through the remains of the building to the ground below. The roaring sound made by the building's collapse was reportedly heard more than a mile away.

About this same time, the State Street Bridge, leading to the North Side, also caught fire, and the inferno began to devour the area on the north side of the river. Soon, stables, warehouses and breweries were also burning. The lumber mills and wood storage yards on the riverbanks were eaten by the fire, and many people who were dunking themselves in the water had to flee again to keep from being strangled by the black smoke. Some people threw chairs and sofas into the river and sat with just their heads and shoulders visible. Many of them stayed in the river for up to fourteen hours.

The flames were not the only threat that the city's residents had to worry about. In the early hours of the fire, looting and violence had broken out. Saloonkeepers, hoping that it might prevent their taverns from being destroyed, had foolishly rolled barrels of whiskey out into the streets. Soon, men and women from all classes were staggering in the streets, thoroughly intoxicated. The drunks and the looters did not comprehend the danger they were in, and many were trampled in the streets. Plundered goods were also tossed aside and lost in the fire, abandoned by the looters as the flames drew near.

Alexander Frear, a New York alderman who was caught in the fire, remembered seeing Wabash Avenue choked with crowds and bundles. He later wrote:

> *Valuable oil paintings, books, pets, musical instruments, toys, mirrors and bedding were trampled underfoot. Goods from stores had been hauled out and had taken fire, and the crowd, breaking into a liquor establishment, was yelling with the fury of demons. A fellow standing on a piano declared that the fire was the friend of the poor man. In this chaos were hundreds of children, wailing and crying for their parents. One little girl in particular I saw, whose golden hair was loose down her back and caught fire. She ran screaming past me and somebody threw a glass of liquor upon her, which flared up and covered her with a blue flame.*

14

Saloonkeepers, hoping that their taverns would not be destroyed, rolled barrels of whiskey into the street. This added to the danger from the fire, since the now intoxicated looters failed to clear the streets for fire vehicles and those running for their lives. *Courtesy of the Library of Congress.*

Frear recalled that everyone seemed to be shouting at the top of their lungs. He saw people pushed off bridges and into the river to drown, while boat crews fought to keep crowds from clambering onto their decks. He wrote that rough-looking men carried women and children to safety and then went back into danger to find more. Police officers saved countless lives, and firemen dashed into the flames and carried out unconscious victims. Horses broke out of stables, or fought loose from their handlers, and ran frenzied through the streets. Rats, smoked out from beneath houses and wooden sidewalks, died squealing under the feet of the fleeing masses.

During the early morning hours, the flames jumped the river to the north, and the panicked residents ran ahead of the fire, edging eastward, toward the lakefront and Lincoln Park. Women's dresses caught on fire. Sick and injured people, carried on mattresses, stretchers and chairs, were knocked to the ground and trampled. Some of the fugitives, insane with fear, plunged into blazing alleyways and were burned alive. Many of the elderly were crushed under the feet of the frantic crowds, and a number of housewives, rushing into their homes for cherished possessions, perished in the inferno. The Chicago Historical Society was destroyed, losing city records of incalculable value and the original draft of the Emancipation Proclamation, which Abraham Lincoln wrote during the Civil War.

Lincoln Park became a macabre location during the fire as it served as a gathering place for uprooted families and fleeing victims. Graves in what had once been the old City Cemetery had been opened so that their occupants could be moved, and now the yawning pits and the haphazardly stacked tombstones were being used to shelter huddled masses of adults and children.

On the lakefront, thousands took refuge away from any buildings that might burn, but they were still tortured by the heat and the storm of falling embers. Men buried their wives and children in the sand, leaving a hole for air, and splashed water over them. Many fled to stand chin-deep in the waters of Lake Michigan, breathing through handkerchiefs.

Throughout the day on Monday, the fire kept to its wind-driven task, finishing the business section and the North Side. The wind blew so hard that firefighters could get water no more than ten feet past the nozzles of their hoses. Fire engines were demolished in the flames, and companies were separated from their officers. The fire department, like the city of Chicago, was destroyed.

Thankfully, the fire began to die on the morning of October 10, when steady and soaking rains began to fall.

The Great Fire, as it was called from then on, was the most disastrous event in America until the San Francisco earthquake and fire of 1906. The people of the city were devastated, as was the city itself. Over 300 people were dead, and the fates of many more were never reported, nor were their bodies found. Another 100,000 were without homes or shelter. The fire had cut a swath through the city that was four miles long and about two-thirds of a mile wide. Over $200 million in property had been destroyed. Records, deeds, archives, libraries and priceless artwork were lost. During the destruction of the Federal Building, which housed, among other things, the post office, more than $100,000 in currency was burned.

Chicago had become a blasted and charred wasteland.

On Tuesday, sightseers poured into town, and among them were hundreds of criminals from neighboring regions, eager for pillage. Local business owners hired Allan Pinkerton to assign his detectives positions around the remains of stores and banks, and soon, six companies of federal troops were deployed under the command of General Phillip Sheridan to assist in maintaining order. Two days later, Chicago's Mayor Roswell Mason placed the city under martial law, entrusting Sheridan and his troops to watch over it.

Sheridan recruited a volunteer home guard of about one thousand men to patrol unburned areas of the city. He also enforced a curfew, much to the chagrin of Illinois governor John M. Palmer, who felt that martial law was uncalled for and unnecessary. Mayor Mason was heavily influenced by local business leaders, however, and ignored Palmer's order to withdraw the troops.

Martial law didn't last long. A few days after it went into effect, a local businessman—one of those responsible for pushing Mason into enacting martial law—was accidentally killed by a member of the volunteer home guard. In spite of this, Sheridan received orders from President Grant that left four companies of men on active duty in the city through the end of the year.

As terrible as the disaster was, Chicago was not dead but merely shaken and stunned. Within days of the fire, rebuilding began on a grand scale. The vigor of the city's rebirth amazed the rest of the nation, and within three years it once again dominated the western United States. It soared from the ashes like the fabled phoenix and became the home of the nation's first skyscraper in 1885. The city passed the one million mark in population five years later. The Great Chicago Fire marked the beginning of a new metropolis, much greater than it could have ever become if the horrific fire had never happened.

The blackened ruins of the West Side afforded people of modest means the chance to start their lives over again. Beginning in the 1880s, waves of immigrant Italians, Russian Jews, Poles and Greeks, escaping poverty and political oppression in their homelands, settled the West Side near what is now the University of Illinois campus. Bohemians, Germans, Lithuanians and Slovaks settled the Lower West Side.

By 1920, it was estimated that 200,000 people lived in the area around Taylor Street and Roosevelt Road. The tragically poor immigrants who eked out an existence in the slums and tenements of this neighborhood coped as best they could with the menace of crime and murder all around them. The entire district was awash in vice. Hoodlums who were driven out of other parts of the city found refuge on the West Side. Bordellos, taverns and drug houses lined the streets. It was to the immigrants trapped in the neighborhood that Jane Addams appealed when she opened her settlement house in the former Charles Hull mansion in 1889, providing education, comfort and an escape from poverty.

Left: A view of some of the immigrant tenement houses that were located along Taylor Street and Roosevelt Road on the city's West Side.

Below: The squalid conditions of the tenements made things miserable for the thousands of immigrants who came to Chicago looking for a better life. Many of them turned to crime as a way to better their stations in life.

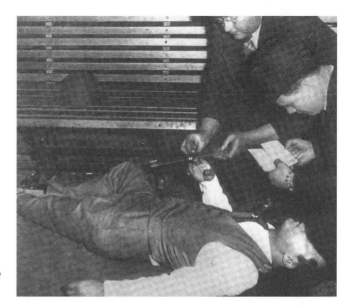

"Machine Gun" Jack McGurn was killed on the anniversary of the St. Valentine's Day Massacre in 1936 in a bowling alley on Milwaukee Avenue. A comic Valentine was left on the dead man's chest. *Courtesy of the* Chicago Daily News.

In the West Town neighborhood, former Al Capone gunman Jack "Machine Gun" McGurn was shot to death in a bowling alley on the seventh anniversary of the St. Valentine's Day Massacre. A group of men, on the pretense of committing a robbery, rushed into the place while McGurn was bowling and killed him on the spot. A comic valentine was left behind on the dead man's body.

In nearby Wicker Park, novelist and poet Nelson Algren once lived among junkies, hustlers and petty criminals and wrote about life on the poor side streets of a neighborhood that is now long gone, replaced by refurbished old buildings that, if they could talk, would have sordid stories to tell. Many of the Prohibition-era taverns in this area were serviced by the Circus Gang, which allegedly supplied the deadly hardware used in the St. Valentine's Day Massacre. As confederates of Al Capone's South Side Outfit, the gang waged a relentless campaign of terror and extortion against tavern owners who refused to buy Capone beer. On April 30, 1929, members of the Circus Gang bombed three saloons on Noble Street, Wabansia Avenue and West North Avenue. Immigrant families lived on the upper floors of all three buildings, and young children were thrown from their beds by the force of the blast. Luckily, no one was killed.

During the years of Prohibition, and during the tenure of Chicago's reform mayor William Dever, mobsters flocked west to Cicero, which was outside the jurisdiction of the Chicago police department and wide open to mob control. Some of the most violent incidents of the so-called "Beer Wars" occurred on the streets of Cicero, and memories of the gangland era are still around today.

This is not the only place on the West Side where frightening memories remain. Near O'Hare International Airport is a quiet neighborhood that holds dark and gruesome secrets. Among the upscale suburban homes there, the legacy of John Wayne Gacy still lingers. His horrific string of crimes seemed impossible to believe, especially by those who saw him as nothing more than a friendly neighbor.

Chicago's West Side has long been a bloody and violent place.

THE MURDER OF AMOS SNELL

Amos Snell is not a name that will be found in most books about Chicago history. Although just as wealthy and successful in business as familiar names like Marshall Field and Potter Palmer, he chose to stay at home and cared nothing for Chicago society. Snell was born in upstate New York and came to Chicago after the Civil War. He earned his millions by buying up unincorporated farmland on the North Side and selling it off as the city began to develop after the war. He used a good part of his fortune to improve the West Side neighborhood where he lived. He had a great dislike of pretentiousness and never attended society events and gatherings. His neighbors knew him as something of a recluse. Nevertheless, his death in 1888 shocked the city.

On a cold night in February, Snell was comfortably in bed, reading a book. The hour was late, and the Norwegian governess, Ida Bjornstad, had just tucked Snell's grandchildren into bed. Snell's wife, Henrietta, and his daughter, Grace Henrietta, were in Milwaukee and were not scheduled to return home for several days. Only Snell, the servants and the children were in the mansion at 425 Washington Boulevard that night. At some point during the early morning hours, an armed intruder broke in through the front door and went down to the basement, where a safe was kept that contained Snell's valuables.

The burglar was not silent when he entered the house. Snell heard a disturbance coming from the downstairs parlor and reached for the gun that he kept at his bedside. Dressed only in his nightclothes, he crept down

The Amos Snell Mansion, located at 425 Washington Boulevard on the city's West Side. *Courtesy of Adam Selzer.*

the stairs and called out to the thieves to leave the house immediately. Upstairs, Rosa Bergstuhler, the German cook, and Ida Bjornstad heard the sound of their employer's voice and realized that someone had broken into the house.

Snell fired blindly into the darkness but only managed to hit a silk decoration and the wall. The burglar returned fire, and Snell was hit in the head and the stomach. He was dead before his body hit the floor. Having already emptied the safe, the thief ran out the front door, carrying away more than $2,000 in cash and bonds.

Snell's body remained in a pool of blood at the bottom of the staircase until it was discovered by the coachman, Henry Winlocke, at dawn. After hearing the shouting and the gunshots, the cook and governess were too afraid to leave their rooms. They locked the doors and stayed in bed, paralyzed with fear, until the police arrived.

Chief of Police Frederick Ebersold was called upon to solve the Snell murder, which could not have come at a worse time. Ebersold was already being criticized for mishandling cases during a recent crime wave. There had been a number of burglaries in the city, all unsolved, and Ebersold was also being held accountable for the public relations fiasco that surrounded the investigation into the 1886 Haymarket Riot bombing. Even though the Snell murder was solved in only eleven days, newspaper editorials pressured the mayor, John A. Roche, to dismiss Ebersold for incompetence. The police department was already badly demoralized, and Ebersold's dismissal made things even more complicated.

When the mayor installed Ebersold's replacement, George W. Hubbard, he promised a speedy resolution of the Snell case. Luckily, he turned out to be right. On February 19, the new superintendent was pleased to announce the name of the man who murdered Amos Snell. Unfortunately, no one was able to find him.

The identity of the killer was learned on the day of Snell's funeral. On that bitterly cold morning, more than three thousand people turned out at the Snell mansion to witness the event, as well as to see the 150 carriages that traveled to Rosehill Cemetery for the interment. One of the carriages in the funeral procession belonged to Mrs. Ella Wick, the owner of a rooming house at 474 West Madison Street. Before departing for the cemetery, Mrs. Wick confided to police detective John Hanley that she had recently rented a room to a young man who called himself William Scott. The man had vacated his room on the morning after the Snell murder, and when asked if he planned to return for his things, he told Mrs. Wick that he would return in two weeks. He asked her to lock the room and keep it for him until he came back.

Mrs. Wick's curiosity had eventually gotten the better of her, and using a passkey, she entered the room to take a look around. She rummaged through the closet and looked under the bed, and she found expensive silverware and other unusual items. Under the bed, she discovered papers that had been taken from the Snell safe. It is unknown why she waited several days before bringing this to the attention of the police.

As investigators began probing into the background of the man, they learned that Scott had recently worked as a night reporter for the *Chicago Times* but was fired for being incompetent. Before that, he had served time at the federal prison in Frankfort, Kentucky, under his real name—William

B. Tascott. It turned out that he was the son of James Tascott, a man of good character and social standing who owned a manufacturing plant on Canal Street. The younger man, who was estranged from his family, was an accomplished thief and con artist.

Information about Tascott was circulated to law enforcement agencies across the Midwest. Trains were searched and passenger lists carefully studied to see if Tascott had purchased a ticket using one of his aliases. Everyone was warned to be on the lookout for a blond-haired man who had scars on his ankles from prison leg irons. A number of leads were followed, but they led nowhere. A possible sighting occurred in St. Paul, Minnesota. The owner of a newsstand spotted a man of Tascott's description, and the suspect claimed to be the advance man for a theatrical company. When the Chicago police went to St. Paul to investigate, the only clue that Tascott had been in the city was his gold-headed cane, which was offered for sale in a pawnshop.

Sightings of the fugitive continued for many years after the murder. The Snell family offered a huge reward for his arrest, but it was never claimed. Every effort was made to track him down, but Tascott simply disappeared into the pages of history. Whatever became of him remains a mystery to this day.

THE BLACK HAND

The Black Hand, an early type of organized crime, was first reported in Chicago about 1900. It became known in a tenement area on the West Side called Smoky Hollow in the 1890s. At that time, Smoky Hollow was a quiet, hardworking community of Irish immigrants that was mostly free of serious crime, except for family squabbles and the occasional clash between rival Irish gangs. By the end of the decade, however, most of the Irish had left the area, and the West Side neighborhood was taken over by poor, working-class Italians. During this next period, when the Italians began to be terrorized by the Black Hand, the neighborhood became known as Little Hell.

During a period that lasted roughly from 1900 to 1920, there were an alleged four hundred murders ascribed to a shadowy entity known as the Black Hand. The gangs that made up the Black Hand preyed on the Italian and Sicilian immigrants who lived along Oak and West Taylor Streets and Grand and Wentworth Avenues. So many murders were committed near the intersection of Milton and Oak Streets that it became popularly known as "Death Corner." This was the favorite killing field of a vicious and mysterious assassin called the "Shotgun Man." He was believed to be responsible for at least one-third of the thirty-eight unsolved murders that occurred between January 1910 and March 1911. Four of the victims were killed during the last three days of that final month.

There were probably as many as sixty or seventy Black Hand gangs at work in Chicago during the first two decades of the twentieth century,

The spot was known as "Death Corner," at the intersection of Oak and Milton Streets. This was the killing field of a notorious murderer known only as the "Shotgun Man." *Courtesy of the* Chicago Daily News.

but all of them appeared to be independent units and the police were never able to connect one with another. Despite the magnitude of their operations, none of the extensive investigations conducted by the police ever revealed a Black Hand organization that reached national, or even citywide, proportions. The Black Hand was not an actual group, it was realized, but a method of crime. It was used by individuals, small groups and large and organized gangs. In Italy and Sicily, it was employed by the Mafia. It was called the Black Hand because, as a general rule, extortion letters, which formed the initial phase of the terrorism, bore the imprint of a hand in black ink, as well as crude drawings of a skull and crossbones or sometimes crosses and daggers.

The way the Black Hand operated was both simple and direct. First, a victim who showed signs of prosperity would be chosen from among the Italian immigrant population. For instance, if a man purchased property and that fact became public knowledge, he could almost always count on the attention of the Black Hand. A letter, bearing a signature of the Black Hand, was sent to the victim demanding money. If the letter was ignored, or the victim refused to pay, his home, office or business would be bombed. If he still refused to pay, he would be murdered. Most of the letters were blunt instructions about sums of money and where they were to be delivered. Others were more clever and worded with politeness and Italian courtesy. No matter how they were phrased, each brought the promise of death if the instructions were not carried out to the letter.

The Black Hand

Dozens of bombs exploded on the West Side in retaliation for nonpayment of extortion. In 1910, the *Chicago Tribune* reported that there were twenty-five unsolved murders connected to the Black Hand. There were forty-three murders in 1911, thirty-three in 1912, thirty-one in 1913 and forty-two in 1914. During the first six months of 1915, six men were killed and twelve bombs were detonated.

As the police attempted to combat the Black Hand gangs, they were faced with impossible obstacles. Hundreds of arrests were made, but suspects were usually released within hours because no evidence connecting them with specific crimes could be secured. Many cases of murder and extortion were brought into the courts, but convictions were nearly impossible to obtain, and those few who were sent to prison were usually quickly paroled thanks to payoffs to corrupt politicians. The reason that it was so hard to prosecute the Black Hand gang leaders was the same reason the gangs were so terrifying in the first place. As soon as a Black Hand suspect was arrested, witnesses and members of the victim's family

Police detectives lead a Black Hand suspect to jail. Unfortunately, most arrests were not effective because members of the shadowy organizations were almost impossible to identify and track down. *Courtesy of the* Chicago Daily News.

were threatened with death if they gave information to the police. Judges, jurors, members of the prosecutor's staff and even their families received threats. In one case, a witness was about to give the details of a Black Hand extortion plot when a man entered the courtroom and waved a red handkerchief at him. The witness froze and refused to speak anymore. The state was forced to abandon the case.

According to the *Chicago Tribune*, "The police, hampered at every turn by the silence of the Italian colony, are compelled to resign themselves to finding nothing. At present, the police acknowledge the futility of further investigation."

By the latter part of the 1910s, police officials were forced to try and downplay the Black Hand. They simply had no way of controlling the situation and no way to combat the threats or apprehend the killers when threats of death were actually carried out. Most Chicago detectives paid the Black Hand criminals a grudging respect as elusive and resourceful prey, while others denied their existence altogether. The prejudices of those in the city government who sought to dismiss the Black Hand failed to take into account the helplessness and despair of the Italian immigrants as they tried to cope with the hardships of life in a new and unpredictable country, only to be faced with being terrorized as well.

Because of this, some of the Italian business and professional men decided to try and take matters into their own hands. They formed what was called the White Hand Society, an organization that was sponsored by wealthy businessmen, the Italian Chamber of Commerce, Italian newspapers and several fraternal orders of Italians and Sicilians. It was formed to work with the police to try to exterminate the Black Hand. Although virtually every member of the society was threatened with death at one time or another, it was active for several years. Private detectives were employed to help the police investigate Black Hand cases, and agents were even sent to Italy and Sicily to look into past histories of the most notorious gangsters. They also arranged for protection for witnesses and their family members. Several murderers and extortionists were sent to prison through the efforts of the White Hand, but they were soon paroled and resumed their activities. For this reason, this society of neighborhood vigilantes was more of a symbolic gesture than anything else. Their intentions were good, but they were up against a much too difficult adversary. The White Hand faded out of existence about 1912.

The Black Hand

The Black Hand endured for about another eight years, until a federal law finally forced the gangs out of existence. Once the federal government began prosecuting extortion as misuse of the United States mail, dozens of Black Hand gangsters began to be convicted, fined and sent to federal prisons. Corrupt politicians were unable to help them, and most of the convicted men served their full sentences. Because of this, Black Hand men were forced to look for other ways to carry out their extortion. By 1920, with the start of Prohibition, most of the extortionist gangs found that bootlegging and rumrunning were greater fields for their talents, and the Black Hand became a thing of the past.

THE DEATH OF FRANK CAPONE

In 1923, the South Side Outfit, run by John Torrio and Al Capone, went looking for a place where it could not only expand its operations but also stay out of the reach of Chicago's new reform mayor, William E. Dever. In just a short time in office, Dever had closed down more than seven thousand speakeasys in the city and had made a sizable dent in the mob's business.

The Outfit found a suitable haven in the West Side town of Cicero. The industrious town, located on the ragged western boundary of Chicago, extending from Roosevelt Road on the north to Pershing Road on the south, was home to about sixty thousand people, and while it had a reputation for being politically corrupt, it was largely a law and order town. The area was dominated by the Western Electric plant, which paid its forty thousand employees well, meaning that the local populace had plenty of money to spend in the gambling parlors and saloons. Cicero also had a large number of Czech immigrants, who were accustomed to thick, Bohemian beer. This was supplied by the West Side O'Donnells, who had not joined the Torrio-Capone syndicate and regarded Cicero as their territory.

Torrio decided to probe the extent of the O'Donnells' power in Cicero by setting up a brothel on Roosevelt Road. The Cicero police, acting for the O'Donnells, shut it down. The city leaders disapproved of prostitution, but they did allow gambling, although only at slot

The Western Electric Plant in Cicero employed almost forty thousand people in the area and paid well, leaving them plenty of money to spend on bootleg liquor and gambling.

Johnny Torrio, the man who brought Al Capone to Chicago and one of the most capable bosses in the history of the outfit. He was the brains behind Capone's violence during the early years of Prohibition. *Courtesy of the* Chicago Daily News.

The Death of Frank Capone

Torrio left Al Capone to handle setting up operations in Cicero. His first test of power came with the city elections of 1924.

machines. The slot machines in Cicero were all controlled by Eddie Vogel, a local politician. Torrio, in retaliation for the brothel closing, sent out the Cook County sheriff to confiscate Vogel's slot machines. Torrio then sat down with the O'Donnells and Vogel and negotiated a truce. The slot machines were returned, and Torrio agreed not to open any more sporting houses in Cicero. In addition, Torrio allowed the O'Donnells to continue supplying beer to some areas of the city. In exchange, the Torrio syndicate was granted the right to sell beer everywhere else in Cicero and to run gambling parlors and dance halls wherever it wanted.

Torrio, having gained entry into Cicero, left everything in Capone's hands and departed for a sightseeing tour of Europe and Italy with his wife and mother. He bought his mother a villa in Naples and deposited a considerable sum of money in various continental banks. He later returned to Chicago, but before that, Capone was left to consolidate their gains in Cicero.

In Torrio's absence, Capone sought a new headquarters and found it at the Hawthorne Inn, located at 4833 Twenty-second Street. It was a two-story structure of brown brick, with white tiles set in the upper façade. Bulletproof steel shutters were fitted for every window, and an armed guard was stationed at each entrance. The interior lobby was dominated by four green columns and mounted big-game heads on the walls. Red-carpeted stairs went up to the second-floor bedrooms, where Capone and his men often spent the night.

The first challenge that awaited Capone in Cicero was taking over the city government. His chance came with the mayoral election of 1924 between Democrat Rudolph Hurt and Republican Joseph Z. Klenha. The Klenha faction, a bipartisan machine, had ruled the town for three terms, but now the Democrats were putting up a separate slate. Worried that Cicero would

Twenty-second Street in Cicero. The Hawthorne Inn is clearly visible. Next door was the Hawthorne Smoke Shop, a gambling parlor that the outfit opened after the 1924 elections.

be infected by the reforms that were taking place in Chicago under Mayor Dever, the Klenha bosses came to Capone with an attractive proposition: if he made sure that Klenha won the election, he could count on immunity from the law in any operation he undertook in Cicero, with the exception of sporting houses. Capone immediately began making plans for election day and borrowed about two hundred men from his Chicago allies to make sure that the vote went Klenha's way. The opposition was also supported by gangsters—rallying bootleg beer wholesalers who wanted to take Torrio-Capone territory for themselves.

The first casualty was the Democratic candidate for town clerk, William K. Pflaum. On March 31, the night before the election, syndicate gangsters raided his campaign headquarters. The place was ransacked, Pflaum's face was bloodied and his wife was shoved against a wall.

On April 1, Capone threw the weight of the syndicate behind Klenha. By this time, Capone had brought his entire family to Chicago, and his brothers, Ralph and Frank, and his cousin, Charley Fischetti, helped bring out the vote for Klenha and other syndicate candidates.

They sowed terror wherever they went. Gangsters stationed themselves at polling booths and made sure that voters only cast ballots for the

The Death of Frank Capone

Capone gunman and cousin Charley Fischetti.

candidates of choice. Those who opposed them were violently beaten, and those who went along were allowed to vote as many times as they wished. Honest poll watchers and election officials were kidnapped and held captive until the polls closed. A Democratic campaign worker named Michael Gavin was shot through both legs and dumped into the basement of a gangster-owned Chicago hotel, along with eight other troublesome Democrats. An election official named Joseph Price was beaten and then kept gagged and tied up at Harry Madigan's Pony Inn. A policeman was blackjacked. Two men were shot dead on Twenty-second Street near the Hawthorne Inn. A third man had his throat cut, and a fourth was killed at Eddie Tancl's saloon.

A group of terrorized Cicero residents appealed for help from Cook County judge Edmund K. Jarecki. He ordered seventy Chicago police officers, five squads of detectives and nine squads of motorized police to go into Cicero and put a stop to the violence. Throughout the afternoon, gangsters and police officers fought pitched battles. The climax of the day came near dusk.

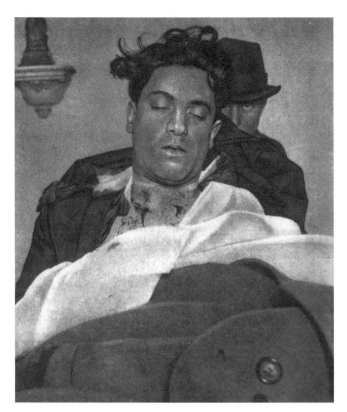

Frank Capone was killed during the violence on election day. He, Al and Charley Fischetti opened fire on a carload of plainclothes detectives who had been dispatched to shut down their actions at a city polling place. The Capones assumed that the cops were rival gangsters. Frank was killed on the spot. *Courtesy of the* Chicago Daily News.

A squad car carrying Detective Sergeant Cusick and Patrolmen McGlynn, Grogan, Cassin and Campion pulled up alongside a polling place at the corner of Twenty-second Street and Cicero Avenue. There, intimidating voters with automatics in their hands, were Al and Frank Capone and Charley Fischetti. The policemen, all dressed in plain clothes, got out of their car with shotguns and rifles and started walking across the street toward the polling place.

The Capones and Fischetti spotted the armed men coming toward them and, mistaking them for rival gangsters, opened fire. Frank Capone took careful aim at Patrolman McGlynn and pulled the trigger—but the automatic didn't fire. Before he could react, McGlynn and Grogan gave him both barrels of their shotguns, and Frank fell to the sidewalk. The police then emptied their revolvers into his body as he lay bleeding on the pavement.

Al Capone, fleeing down the sidewalk, ran into another squad and managed to hold them at bay with a gun in each hand until he could vanish under the cover of darkness. The police never arrested him. They captured Fischetti, but he was released a short time later.

Frank Capone, only twenty-nine years old, was given a magnificent gangland funeral. He was placed in a silver-plated casket, and the modest Capone home on South Prairie Avenue was filled with more than $20,000 worth of flowers. A procession of one hundred cars took the casket to Mount Carmel Cemetery. In Cicero, as a mark of respect for the slain man, nearly every tavern owner kept his blinds drawn and his doors locked for two hours.

One month after the elections, Torrio and Capone launched, without interference, their first Cicero gambling den, the Hawthorne Smoke Shop, next to the Hawthorne Inn. Capone had lost a brother, but he had won the election. The mob was now in charge of Cicero.

THE HOUSE OF WEIRD DEATH

The street where the Wynekoop Mansion was once located is a crime-ridden and forlorn area on Chicago's West Side. It was once a place of opulence and prestige, but it is now a scene of silent desolation. The weather-beaten old homes stand with an almost ghostlike presence that hearkens back to days of past elegance. The Wynekoop Mansion was destroyed many years ago, but its memory and reputation still linger today. It is best remembered for its notorious nickname, the "House of Weird Death."

Drs. Frank and Alice Wynekoop built the mansion at 3406 West Monroe Street in 1901. They closely supervised the construction, planning to turn the red brick home into a safe and loving environment for their family. The house seemed to be a warm and welcoming place for a time, but then events conspired to make words like "haunted" and "cursed" better adjectives to describe the place. The house was marked by death, illness and scandal, but no single occurrence affected the house like the death of Rheta Wynekoop in 1933.

In the years before this horrific event, the mansion was a wonderful place for the Wynekoops. Two sons and a daughter were added to the family, and later, another daughter was added, this time by adoption. All of the children, who brought Alice many years of happiness, thrived in the environment of learning and respect that was fostered in the family home. Their only sadness came with the death of Dr. Frank Wynekoop while the children were still young.

The brownstone Wynekoop Mansion, which came to be known as the "House of Weird Death" in the sensational newspaper stories of the day. *Courtesy of* True Detective *magazine.*

The House of Weird Death

The charming
and treacherous
Earle Wynekoop.
Courtesy of True
Detective *magazine.*

The children were raised by their mother, Dr. Alice Lindsay Wynekoop. She was an early advocate of women's rights and a promoter of the suffrage movement. In addition to being a graduate of the Women's Medical School at Northwestern University, she was a pillar of the community and was much loved and admired for her charitable deeds and work on behalf of those in need. She was also a civic leader and a pioneer in the movement for children's health. Dr. Alice maintained her office in her home, in a basement suite that was built for that purpose, accessible from West Monroe Street.

Her children continued to bring her joy as they grew into adults. Her oldest son, Walker, became a respected businessman in Wilmette, married and had two children of his own. Catherine, the youngest of the family, also studied medicine and became a surgeon and a highly respected member of the staff of the Cook County Hospital. The pride of Dr. Wynekoop's life, however, was her son Earle. Other members of the family saw him as a lazy playboy who did anything he could to avoid actual work. He was an embarrassment to the rest of the family, but Dr. Alice never saw this side of him. Despite his many faults, he doted on his mother, using every ounce of charm that he could muster.

At the age of twenty-seven, Earle was still being supported by his mother and residing in her fashionable brownstone. By this time, his younger sister was finishing her medical training and his brother had married and settled in Wilmette. Earle was living a carefree life of travel, and while visiting Indianapolis, he met an attractive, redheaded heiress named Rheta Gardner. She was an entertainer at a concert he attended, and when he returned to Chicago, he began corresponding with her. Less than a year later, he coaxed her into coming to Chicago and convinced her that they should be married. Since Rheta was only eighteen, Alice insisted that Earle obtain consent for the marriage from the girl's father, an Indianapolis flour and salt merchant named Burdine H. Gardner. It was given somewhat grudgingly, but Gardner wanted his daughter to be happy so he agreed to attend the wedding.

A celebration was held at the house on the day of the wedding, but Rheta refused to spend her wedding night in the Wynekoop mansion. After a night

Earle's lovely and ill-fated wife, Rheta Gardner Wynekoop. *Courtesy of* True Detective *magazine.*

in a hotel, she and Earle left on their honeymoon. While they were away, Alice redecorated and refinished a suite of rooms on the second floor so that it would be ready for the newlyweds when they returned.

Rheta came home to the mansion and took her place among the rather unusual group of people residing there, including her husband, who made no plans to look for employment now that he was married. The other occupants of the house included Dr. Alice Wynekoop, her mother-in-law, and her sister-in-law Catherine, who was studying to become a doctor. There was Marie Louise, the adopted daughter, a shadowy and unfortunate young girl who lived a short life. There was also Miss Catherine Porter, a woman of about Alice's age who was rooming there and being treated by Alice for cancer and heart disease and who also shared a bank account with her doctor and devoted friend. There was also another tenant named Miss Enid Hennessey, a middle-aged schoolteacher who shared rooms with her elderly father. It was a strange place, filled with mostly eccentric people, and it must have been overwhelming for the young Rheta.

After the couple returned to Chicago, Rheta was largely abandoned by Earle, who had quickly lost interest in the pretty young woman. He was rarely at home, and Rheta was forced to make the best of a bad situation, stranded in Alice's dark and gloomy mansion, playing her violin. She was an accomplished musician and hoped to one day pursue music as a career.

In the meantime, the only thing that Earle was pursuing was a string of young women. His black book contained the names of more than fifty young women whom he had wooed and bedded during the 1933 World's Fair. The handsome rake had proposed marriage to several of the poor, lovesick young girls who worked at concession stands on the fairgrounds. He escorted them about the fair, buying them food and small trinkets and whispering of the future they would have together. He took special care to avoid areas of the fair where his other sweethearts might be working. According to reports, when the details of Earle's many affairs were later revealed, his numerous fiancées accused him of making love to them in strange ways that were "shocking and repulsive."

Earle's bizarre behavior just made things worse for Rheta. Since the time of the wedding and the couple's subsequent return to Chicago, she had become more and more unhappy. She had been all but forgotten by her handsome husband and had been left with the companionship of her aging mother-in-law and a middle-aged schoolteacher. The only bright spots in her life were her music and the friendship of her "sisters," Marie Louise and Catherine. A series of deaths occurred in the house over a short period of time. Marie

Louise, the adopted daughter, died suddenly, followed by Dr. Alice's friend Miss Porter. A few days later, the elderly father of Miss Hennessey also passed away. Soon after, Catherine became a resident physician at Cook County Hospital and moved out of the Wynekoop Mansion for good.

Rheta plunged into depression, a condition of which she was mortally afraid. When she was only seven years old, her mother had been confined to an insane asylum and had died there, some ten years later, from tuberculosis. Because of this, Rheta had a great fear of illness and an even greater fear of going insane herself. One cannot help but wonder what was going through her mind as she wandered around the old mansion each day, wondering where her husband was spending his nights and what would become of her in the future. Sadly, she would not wonder about her future for long.

On November 21, 1933, at about 10:00 p.m., police officers from the Fillmore Street Station were summoned to the Wynekoop Mansion on West Monroe Street. The officer in charge of squad car 15 later reported:

> We went directly there and were met at the front door by a lady who told us to come inside. The lady we met first we later found to be Miss Enid Hennessey, a schoolteacher and roomer there. When we got inside, we met the defendant, Dr. Wynekoop. She was seated in a chair in the library. Mr. Ahearn, an undertaker, was there. We asked the defendant what happened. She said "something terrible has happened; come on downstairs and I will show you."

The officers found Rheta lying facedown on Dr. Alice's emergency operating table in the basement. She was partially nude, and she had a bullet wound in her back, just under her left shoulder. Next to the body, they found a chloroform mask and the murder weapon. Three shots had been fired, and the gun had been left lying next to the girl's head.

The crowd of police attracted onlookers outside and made things very tense inside the house. Detectives, who soon arrived on the scene, began questioning everyone, including Dr. Alice. As she began speaking, she continually changed her story, confusing the police, the coroner and even members of the household. Many wondered if the beloved doctor might be incoherent over the girl's death. She advanced the theory that Rheta may have killed herself in a fit of depression and then suggested that a burglar was responsible for the crime, declaring that both money and drugs were missing from the house. But to Captain John Stege, the manner of Rheta's death didn't agree with the theory of a burglar. He had also ruled out suicide because of the angle of the shot and the chloroform burns present on the girl's face.

There was a lot that Captain Stege needed to know and, as word leaked out about the murder, a lot that the public and press wanted to know, as well. For instance, where was Earle Wynekoop on the night of the murder?

According to Earle's version of events, he was traveling west to photograph the Grand Canyon for the Santa Fe Railroad, accompanied by a friend named Stanley, at the time of his wife's death. He claimed that he had started west for Arizona several days before the murder, but rumor had it that he had been seen in Chicago not more than a day before the crime. He was taken into custody when he arrived from Kansas City by train. He was not accompanied by a friend named Stanley but by an attractive young girl whom he had met at the fair. She knew him as Michael Wynekoop, and he

Dr. Alice Wynekoop at the time of Rheta's murder. *Courtesy of* True Detective *magazine.*

had told her that he was not married. She was soon released, but Earle was taken in for questioning.

Reports stated that he was cooperative with the police interviews and gave an opinion that "a moron" had murdered Rheta. He added other, even more interesting, details about his married life. The marriage, Earle said, was a failure. On one occasion, Rheta had attempted to poison the family by putting iron fillings and drugs in their food. She had tuberculosis, he added, and was mentally deranged.

While Earle was making wild and far from helpful statements to the press and police, Rheta's father, Burdine H. Gardner, was rushing to Chicago. He met with Dr. Alice and then dramatically took his daughter's body home for burial. Dr. Alice insisted that he tell everyone that Rheta's death had been caused by complications from tuberculosis. He later stated that he found the living arrangements at the Wynekoop house to be rather odd, and Dr. Alice even more so. "She struck me as a most peculiar person," he told a newspaper reporter.

The police continued the investigation. Confused by the large and eccentric collection of characters who lived in the house, they began questioning all of them, including Dr. Alice. They turned out to be a bizarre group, each one fiercely loyal to Dr. Alice. When detectives hinted to Miss Hennessey that Alice might have been responsible for Rheta's death, she became hysterical and began screaming, "It's a lie! It's a lie!" She stood faithfully by the doctor through the trial that followed and even invented an alibi to protect her friend.

Dr. Alice continued to invent her own stories to explain her daughter-in-law's death. Her "burglars" became "drug fiends." In recent months, she claimed, her basement office had been broken into and drugs had been stolen. She suggested that Rheta might have caught them in the act. Detectives grilled Alice for hours, but she refused to say or do anything to incriminate herself or Earle. Eventually, detectives told her that they had just learned that Earle had taken out a $5,000 life insurance policy on Rheta, so he must have been the killer.

At that point, she confessed.

Her concern for Earle finally caused Dr. Alice to break. She confessed that she, not Earle, had pulled the trigger, but only after Rheta had already expired from deadly anesthetic. Dr. Wynekoop explained that she had been about to perform a painful surgical procedure on the young woman. She said that she had asked Rheta to pour some chloroform into the mask to ease the pain of the surgery, but the dosage had proven to be too much.

Minutes later, the girl had lapsed into a coma. Fearing public humiliation and a ruined reputation, Dr. Alice had panicked and fired the fatal shot into the girl. She then blamed the crime on imaginary drug fiends.

The sensational confession raised doubts among the detectives. They still believed that "charming" Earle had masterminded the crime and his mother had taken the blame for it to save her "little boy." Love letters between the mother and son revealed a relationship that went well beyond the norm. One such letter became public; it had been written after a secret meeting between Alice and Earle on the Sunday evening before the murder. Assistant State's Attorney Charles S. Doughtery believed that Alice had made up her mind to murder Rheta after this meeting. No one actually knows what was said at that meeting—and never will—but after her return home, Alice wrote Earle a frantic note that read:

> *Sunday night—*
> *Precious—*
> *I'm choked—you are gone—you have called me up—and after 10 minutes or so, I called and called—no answer—maybe you are sleeping—you need to be—but I want to hear your voice again tonight—I would give anything I had—to spend an hour—in real talk with you—tonight—and I cannot—Good night.*

But why would Dr. Alice have killed Rheta? Was she jealous of Rheta's relationship with her son? State's Attorney Doughtery believed that there was another girl, one whom Earle truly loved and who was not Rheta or his mother. Earle had given this girl a diamond engagement ring, said to have been the one he had previously given to Rheta. For religious reasons, neither his family nor the family of the girl believed in divorce.

Doughtery cited this as a motive for the murder, with a demented Alice trying to ensure the happiness of her son by getting rid of his unwanted wife. He also added that Alice was deeply in debt, and by killing Rheta, she could collect on an insurance policy that she had taken out on the girl.

After hearing of his mother's confession, Earle made five obviously false confessions of his own, culminating in a wild story about how he had slipped into the Wynekoop home on Tuesday afternoon, hid in the basement for his wife, seized her, threw her onto the operating table, killed her and then fled by airplane to Kansas City. He tried to reenact how he had done all of this but so badly bungled the "crime" that detectives actually laughed at him. Needless to say, his entire story was dismissed and his confession debunked

The cover of one of the wildly sensational pulp magazines of the day that covered the Wynekoop murder case.

when it was proven that his alibi was intact. He really was out of state at the time of the murder. Prosecutors still believed that Dr. Alice was responsible for the murder, killing Rheta because she needed money and hated her daughter-in-law for making her son so miserable.

The Wynekoop case stayed in the newspaper headlines for months. On November 28, Dr. Alice became seriously ill with a bronchial cough and high blood pressure. From her sickbed in the prison hospital, she reversed her confession and claimed that the police had coerced her into making it after sixty hours of questioning. During that time, she said, she had been given no food or drink, save for a single cup of coffee. Two days later, she changed her story again and this time stated that she had only made the confession because she did not think she would live to stand trial.

The House of Weird Death

The trial was scheduled for January, but in the meantime the Wynekoops stayed in the public eye. On December 2, Earle announced that the family had hired a private detective to solve the mystery and prove his mother's innocence. Apparently, nothing ever came of the investigation for it was never spoken of again.

A few days later, newspapers carried reports that Rheta's body had been exhumed in Indianapolis, and the coroner announced that there was no trace of chloroform in her body, thus repudiating one portion of Alice's story.

In the middle of December, two events occurred that, while having nothing to do with Rheta's murder, managed to keep the Wynekoops in the headlines. On December 14, Earle ran over a nine-year-old boy with his automobile. His sister, Dr. Catherine Wynekoop, was in the car with him at the time. Shortly after, Alice's brother-in-law, Dr. Gilbert Wynekoop, was found to be mentally deranged by a jury that was trying him for attacking a nurse. He was sent to St. Luke's Hospital for the Insane.

These happenings helped to put Chicago into a state of great excitement by the time Dr. Alice's trial opened in January. The case dragged on for weeks, attracting great public attention. Nearly six months after the weird murder, on March 6, 1934, a jury returned a verdict of guilty against the doctor. The press and the public were strongly divided over whether justice had been served with the verdict. Alice was sentenced to twenty-five years in prison but was granted parole from the Women's Reformatory in Dwight in 1949. She was seventy-nine years old, and she died two years later, her life and reputation destroyed.

The rest of the family managed to survive the disgrace of the murder and trial. Walter Wynekoop went on to a successful business career, and Catherine became an esteemed physician, long associated with the Children's Clinic of the Cook County Hospital. Only Earle vanished completely from the public eye. In 1945, he was working as an auto mechanic, but that was the last time anyone heard from him. Most likely, he died many years ago.

The "House of Weird Death," as the newspapers called it, was torn down many decades ago. The neighborhood itself, the Fillmore district, is now a crime-ridden area. Where graceful mansions once stood, only empty lots remain. Rheta Wynekoop, along with the rest of this strange clan, is now long forgotten.

John Hamilton's Mysterious Death

Little is known about the life of John "Red" Hamilton prior to his criminal career and his association with famed bank robber John Dillinger. Perhaps even less is known about what happened to him following the ill-fated FBI raid on the lodge known as Little Bohemia in April 1934. Despite an astonishing lack of evidence, speculation about his death runs rampant, and rumors persist about where he died, if he died at all, and whose body was buried west of Chicago.

"Red" Hamilton (who was also sometimes known as "Three-Fingered Jack") was a small-time hood from Canada when he lucked into meeting John Dillinger while serving time at the Indiana State Prison in Michigan City. On March 16, 1927, he was convicted of robbing a gas station in St. Joseph, Indiana, and sentenced to twenty-five years. While incarcerated, Hamilton became friends with a number of prominent bank robbers, including John Dillinger, Russell Clark, Charles Makley, Harry Pierpont and Homer Van Meter—the men who would go on to make up the original Dillinger gang.

Dillinger was paroled in May 1933 but swore that he would break his friends out of prison. Using a list that had been compiled by Hamilton and Pierpont, Dillinger began robbing banks to finance the escape. In September of that same year, he managed to get a barrel filled with guns smuggled into the penitentiary, and a total of ten armed men, including Hamilton, escaped out the front gates.

John "Red" Hamilton, one of the original members of the Dillinger gang. *Courtesy of the Library of Congress.*

Soon after they escaped, the gang learned that Dillinger had been arrested and was being held at the Allen County Jail in Lima, Ohio. Determined to free him, they, in turn, needed cash to finance the escape and robbed the First National Bank in St. Mary's, Ohio, on October 3, 1933. They escaped with $14,000. Nine days later, Hamilton accompanied Charles Makley, Harry Pierpont, Russell Clark and Ed Shouse to the Lima jail, where Dillinger was being held. However, Hamilton did not go inside and did not participate in the murder of Sheriff Jess Sarber, for which Makley and Pierpont would later be convicted.

Over the course of the next couple of months, Hamilton took part in a number of daring robberies with Dillinger and the rest of the gang. After a profitable robbery in Wisconsin, the gang went down to Florida for a time and then west to Tucson. Hamilton instead decided to go to Chicago, where, on December 13, 1933, he took part in the robbery of a local bank. A day earlier, Hamilton had left his car at a Chicago garage for some bodywork. For some reason, the garage's mechanic called the police with his suspicion that the vehicle was a "gangster's car." When Hamilton returned to pick up the car, he was confronted by Sergeant William Shanley and two other officers. Hamilton opened fire, killing Shanley, and managed to elude capture by the other officers.

Meanwhile, Dillinger and the others had been apprehended by the authorities in Tucson, leading to disaster for several members of the gang. A short time later, Dillinger managed to escape from the Crown Point, Indiana jail and mustered a new gang, which included Hamilton, Homer Van Meter, Tommy Carroll, Eddie Green and George "Baby Face" Nelson.

Hamilton subsequently accompanied the gang on a string of lucrative but chaotic bank robberies, including a heist that resulted in Hamilton being wounded. The robbery occurred at a bank in Mason City, Iowa, that allegedly had over $240,000 in its vault. The gang arrived at the bank on March 13, 1934. Nelson stayed with the getaway car while, inside the bank, the rest of the gang ran into one problem after another. When the bank president, Willis Bagley, saw Van Meter walk in carrying a machine gun, he thought that a "crazy man was on the loose." He ran into his office and bolted the door. Van Meter, knowing that Bagley had the keys to the vault, fired a number of shots through the door but gave up trying to break in and helped his associates clean out the teller drawers.

Moments later, a guard in a special steel cage above the lobby fired a tear gas shell at Eddie Green. It hit him in the back and almost knocked him down. As he swung around, he fired his machine gun, and several bullets clipped the guard.

At the same time, a female customer, who was missing a shoe, ran out of the bank and down the alley outside, where she ran directly into a short man wearing a cap. She begged him to call for help—the bank was being robbed. Unfortunately for her, the short man was Baby Face Nelson, and he sent her back into the bank.

Meanwhile, John Hamilton was having his own problems. Cashier Harry Fisher had barricaded himself in the room with the vault. Since Hamilton could not open the door, he ordered Fisher to start passing money to him through a slot in the door. Fisher began handing him stacks of one-dollar bills.

Dillinger was outside, guarding prisoners on the street. An elderly policeman named John Shipley spotted him from his third-floor office and took a shot at him. He winged Dillinger on the arm, and the bank robber whirled around and fired a burst from his machine gun. The bullets bounced off the front of the building, and Shipley ducked away unhurt. With that, Dillinger decided that it was time to leave. He sent Van Meter inside to get the others.

Hamilton was still having problems with Cashier Fisher. He could see the stacks of bills on the shelves inside the vault where Fisher stood. He demanded that the man open the door, but Fisher told him that he couldn't do it without the key. Hamilton continued to threaten him with his gun, and Fisher continued to load stacks of one-dollar bills into the bandit's bag. He was enraged when Van Meter came inside and told him that they were leaving, as he had only about $20,000 in his bag and there was over $200,000 still sitting in the vault. Gritting his teeth in frustration, he turned and ran out of the bank, leaving the crafty Fisher to count his blessings. Hamilton later said that he should have shot the man, just out of spite.

At the same moment Hamilton ran out of the bank to join the others, Officer Shipley returned to the overhead window and started shooting again. He wounded Hamilton in the shoulder, but the bank robber managed to get to where Dillinger and the others were waiting. They forced twenty hostages to stand on the running boards, fenders and hood of the getaway car, serving as human shields. The bank robbers piled inside and drove slowly away, the car groaning and creaking under all of the extra weight. The police were unable to shoot or try and stop them with all of the hostages on the vehicle, so they were forced to follow at a distance. A few miles out of town, Nelson climbed out of the car and fired his machine gun in their direction, finally forcing the police to turn back. After following back roads at slow speeds for more than two hours, Dillinger dropped off the reluctant passengers and headed for St. Paul. What should have been a prosperous raid had netted the outlaws a disappointing $52,000.

After a close call with the authorities in St. Paul, Hamilton and Dillinger made a discreet visit to Hamilton's sister's house in Sault Sainte Marie, Michigan, on April 17. Looking for a place to lie low for a while, Pat Reilly, a fringe member of the group, told Dillinger about a quiet Wisconsin resort he knew of called Little Bohemia. It was a remote fishing camp that was not due to open until May and would make the perfect place to hide out for a time. Over the next day or two, the gang drove into the Wisconsin woods and checked into the Little Bohemia Lodge to plan its next robbery.

Little Bohemia seemed to be just the answer for the gang, but somebody talked. Soon, Melvin Purvis, the head of the FBI office in Chicago, received a tip from a rival resort owner in Rhinelander, Wisconsin, that Dillinger

Little Bohemia Lodge in Wisconsin, the site of the April 1934 shootout between the Dillinger gang and federal agents. Only the gangsters' wives and girlfriends were captured, and the FBI managed to kill or wound three visiting outdoorsmen. *Courtesy of the Library of Congress.*

was at Little Bohemia. Within hours, Purvis moved dozens of agents from Chicago and St. Paul to the forests of Wisconsin. They planned a raid on the lodge for April 22, 1934.

On the night of the assault, Purvis moved his agents into position at the front of the lodge just as three men emerged and climbed into a parked car. As the engine started, Purvis shouted for the men to stop, but they never heard his warning. Seconds later, FBI agents unleashed a hail of gunfire and ripped the car apart. Eugene Boiseneau, a Civilian Conservation Corps worker, was killed instantly, and his two fishing buddies were both wounded.

Hearing the gunfire outside, Dillinger, Van Meter, Carroll and Hamilton ran out the back of the lodge and disappeared into the woods along the lake. Baby Face Nelson, who was staying in a nearby cabin with his wife, ran outside, fired some random shots at the agents and also vanished into the trees.

Purvis, believing that Dillinger was still inside the lodge, ordered the assembled agents to continue firing into the building. They pounded the lodge all night long, shattering windows and splintering the walls, floors and ceilings with bullets. When morning came, and there was no resistance, they entered the building to capture the gang's girls, who had been hiding in the basement all night.

While FBI agents were pouring more than one thousand bullets and thousands of pellets of buckshot into the empty floors of Little Bohemia, Dillinger and the gang were stealing cars at neighboring farms and resorts and heading off in different directions. Nelson killed one federal agent and wounded another, as well as a local officer, at a nearby resort. Tommy Carroll eluded everyone, and Dillinger, Hamilton and Van Meter stayed together.

In Park Falls, Wisconsin, the trio commandeered a Ford coupe and headed toward St. Paul. They ran into Rusk County sheriff Carl Nelson at the Flambeau River Bridge near Ladysmith, Wisconsin, and Van Meter managed to slip past the sheriff and his deputies long enough to hit Wisconsin Route 46, cross the Mississippi River and enter Minnesota at Red Wing. On U.S. 61, they headed for St. Paul. The tired gangsters were not thinking clearly and were heading back to the same city from which they had escaped before. The authorities were thinking much faster, and Dakota County deputies spotted the trio's Wisconsin license plates on a bridge at Hastings, just fifteen miles from St. Paul. Officers gave chase, only to be blocked by a slow-moving cattle truck on the two-lane bridge. Once they could pass, they managed to track down the blue Ford about ten miles farther north at St. Paul Park.

Deputy Norman Deiter leaned out the window with a .30-30 rifle and fired at one of the Ford's rear tires. The slug punched through the thin body of the automobile between the fender and the spare, tore through the rear seat and drilled into John Hamilton's back. He screamed in agony and was slammed forward against the front seat of the car.

Dillinger smashed out the window behind Hamilton and returned fire with his .45, shattering the windshield of the police car just above Deputy Joe Heinen's head. The daring officers stayed with the fleeing vehicle, and the two cars traded forty or fifty rounds for the next fifty miles or so, until finally the bandits managed to lose the cops about two miles from where the chase started. They continued their journey, doubling back through St. Paul Park and crossing the Mississippi River once again.

With Hamilton losing blood from the gaping wound in his back, and the local police surely on to them by now, Dillinger decided to head to Chicago and find a doctor for his friend. First, though, they would need a faster and less-recognizable vehicle. Van Meter cut off a 1934 Ford V8 Deluxe at City Road 10 and Fifth Avenue. Power company manager Roy Francis, his wife, Sybil, and their nineteen-month-old son, Robert, were ordered out of the car as the bandits tossed their belongings into the flashy roadster. After the injured Hamilton managed to get himself inside, Dillinger ordered the Francis family back inside, as well. Sybil Francis recognized Dillinger right away, but he smiled at her reassuringly. He told her, "Don't worry about the kid. We like kids."

Van Meter followed in the other car to Robert Street and Willy Road, where the slower, bullet-riddled Ford was dumped. The Francis family was dropped off a short time later, a few miles outside of Mendota. The bandits wished them well and continued on toward Chicago.

When they arrived in the city, Dillinger desperately tried to find a doctor to treat his failing friend. The wound in Hamilton's back, which was the size of a silver dollar, was festering and starting to stink of gangrene. They managed to track down the unscrupulous Dr. Joseph Moran, the greedy practitioner who was well known for treating underworld characters and had previously hit up Dillinger for $5,000 after caring for wounds from an earlier robbery. This time, though, Moran refused to ___ services at any price, possibly because he knew that Hamilton would ___ recover from his wound. Moran suggested that they take Hamilton to Elmer's Tavern in Bensenville and let him die there. Hamilton, his agony increasing by the hour, spent a few days at Elmer's, but he simply didn't die. Finally, Dillinger took him to a Barker-Karpis gang safe house in Aurora at 415 Fox Street. The place was being rented by gangster Volney Davis and his girlfriend, Edna "Rabbits" Murray. Edna took care of Hamilton as best she could, but he was a lost cause. Ravaged with gangrene and stinking up the house, Hamilton finally died on Thursday, April 26.

Dillinger, Van Meter, Volney Davis and some of the Barker-Karpis crew buried Hamilton in a gravel pit near Oswego, Illinois, covering the body with ten cans of watered-down lye to make identification more difficult. Dillinger delivered a eulogy: "Sorry, old friend, to have to do this. I know you'd do as much for me." Davis placed a roll of rusty wire that he found nearby on the grave as a makeshift marker.

John Hamilton was left there to rest in peace—or so the story went. Legend, however, tells many different tales about his eventual fate.

Hamilton supposedly died in Aurora at the house that had been rented to Volney Davis. His girlfriend, Edna, had been ordered out of the house before Hamilton died and did not hear about his death and subsequent Oswego burial until she reunited with Davis later that year.

As far as the FBI knew, and despite the blood that was liberally splashed around the backseat of the abandoned Ford coupe, Hamilton's death was still uncertain, based on second- and third-hand accounts of those connected with Dillinger. None of the people who talked had actually been there to see Hamilton die, and all seemed to have different stories to tell. One rumor claimed that Hamilton had been buried in the sand dunes of northern Indiana. Another claimed that he had been weighted down and dropped into an abandoned mine shaft in Wisconsin. It was not until Davis had been arrested, escaped and arrested again that FBI agents learned of the unsuccessful efforts of Dillinger and Van Meter to get medical treatment for Hamilton from Dr. Joseph Moran.

It is possible that Hamilton persisted. After Dillinger was killed on July 22, his girlfriend, Polly Hamilton (no relation to John), said that Anna Sage had told her that Hamilton was being treated for a "badly infected wound" by Dr. Harold Cassidy. If this were true, Hamilton was alive as of June 1934 and possibly later.

Nevertheless, Volney Davis, and others, stuck to the story that Hamilton had died in agony at the Aurora safe house, and he provided a general description of the burial site. There were inconsistencies of the actual time and place of Hamilton's death and the persons involved in the burial, but more than a year later, on August 28, 1935, federal agents went digging in an Oswego gravel pit and found a badly decomposed body.

Before the body was found, the FBI had been receiving reports from police and individuals claiming that John Hamilton was alive and hiding out in northern Indiana. Since he had been reported killed on other occasions, the search continued until the body was found in Oswego, minus a hand and so corroded from the lye that had been poured over it that the agents had little to identify the corpse besides some strands of hair and a belt size. The best they could do was to pull a few molars from the skull and send them to the physician at the Indiana state prison. The physician compared them to Hamilton's dental chart, which showed some fillings, and declared that the FBI had found their man. This satisfied J. Edgar Hoover, who proclaimed the belated discovery of the last member of the Dillinger gang to every newspaper in the country. The case of John Hamilton was now officially closed.

The body that was taken from the gravel pit was buried in the Oswego cemetery, and the funeral service was paid for by Hamilton's sister from Michigan. But was Hamilton really dead?

Reports claiming that Hamilton was still alive continued coming in to the FBI on a regular basis, but they were apparently disregarded. Most could be written off as cases of mistaken identity, but at least one of them was particularly convincing. The letter was recorded by the FBI on August 24, 1936 (a year after Hamilton's body was supposedly found). It was sent by a former prisoner who was known as "Happy." He knew some of the gang members, as well as Arthur O'Leary, an investigator for Dillinger's attorney, Louis Piquett. It is believed that "Happy" may have been an associate of Dillinger named Fred Meyers, who lived in Chicago. The letter read:

> *Dear Sir:*
>
> *Will you kindly advise how much you will guarantee in cash secret and confidential information about the movements of John Hamilton? There are three people who know that he is still living and happen to know the details concerning him.*
>
> *If interested please make offer through personal column of* Chicago Tribune *as follows, HAP *Will buy, 000 bushels, meaning of course that many thousand dollars for this information and place ED after the word bushels. If this offer is OK you will be supplied with an amazing detail report on his present physical condition and movements. Money must be on deposit at your Chicago Office but will not have to be paid until this man is captured or killed or both. This information must be kept strictly confidential between you and I and must be kept out of the newspapers except code transmissions between you and I. I am a hard working electrician and took considerable time and money to get this data and do not want to risk my life for the deal. Everything will be handled by correspondence and code in the* Chicago Tribune. *If your offer is accepted, I will make you proposals which must be guaranteed by you as a strictly gentlemen's agreement.*

The FBI received the letter, but there is nothing to indicate that J. Edgar Hoover ever saw it. There was likely no follow-up ever done because by the time the body believed to be Hamilton was found, Hoover had won the national "War on Crime," appeared on the cover of *Time* magazine and was turning his attention to the communist threat.

Could the letter writer have been telling the truth? There are many who believe so. One of those who became convinced that John Hamilton survived his wounds and was never buried in Oswego was a nephew, Bruce

Hamilton. Many years after the fact, Bruce described a trip taken by family members in 1945 that resulted in the collection of a large amount of money. He was later told that the money had been stashed away by the Dillinger gang, the whereabouts of which was known to the gang's only surviving member, John Hamilton.

After the trip was over, Bruce's father, Wilton Hamilton, paid off the mortgage on his home in South Bend, Indiana, bought a new house and purchased the family's first new car.

Less than a year later, Wilton planned a trip to Sault Sainte Marie on the Canadian border to see relatives at the home of John Hamilton's sister, Anna. The journey was made by Wilton and his wife, Harriet; their older son, Douglas; their daughter, Jane Margaret; and Bruce, then fifteen years old. It was during this trip, which centered on a gathering of about a dozen relatives, that Bruce met the man he was told afterward was his relative John Hamilton. He and his brother and sister were told not to discuss the trip with anyone.

About this same time, Hamilton's brother, Foye, who had been recently released from prison, came into a great deal of money. He used it to build a machine shop in Rockford, Illinois, and he also purchased Turtle Island in the Great Lakes area near Sault Sainte Marie, as well as boats and a seaplane to use getting to and from the island. Bruce suspected that a large cabin on the island provided a hiding place for his uncle John.

Bruce's interest in John Hamilton increased with age, and he learned more details about what had happened to him from his father. Apparently, the wounded Hamilton, after stopping in Aurora and then Chicago (where the FBI originally believed he had died), obtained treatment from Dr. Cassidy and went into hiding with his brother, Sylvester, in East Gary, Indiana. Dillinger then returned to Aurora, while Sylvester took John to the home of William Hamilton, Bruce's grandfather, in South Bend. William helped get him to a hideout previously used by the Dillinger gang, a nearby place called Rum Village Woods. Hamilton recuperated well enough to go to work as an electrician at a family-owned bowling alley in South Bend in 1936 and 1937. According to an elderly aunt of Bruce Hamilton, John later moved to Canada and died in the 1970s.

But if John Hamilton didn't die in Aurora in 1934, then whose body was disinterred in Oswego in 1935? One possibility is that the body belonged to Dr. Joseph Moran, who disappeared shortly after refusing to treat Hamilton's wound in Chicago. Hoover and the FBI had pursued Moran for months after he vanished, and later declared that he had been killed and dumped in Lake Michigan. Alvin Karpis, one of the leaders of the infamous Barker-Karpis gang, would only say that Moran had been murdered and buried, but he would not say where.

Was the decomposed corpse found in the gravel pit Dr. Moran? And if so, did John Hamilton really survive his alleged death? These are two mysteries that will likely never be solved.

THE BATTLE OF BARRINGTON

One of the most terrifying gunfights to ever take place in Illinois history occurred in the town of Barrington on Chicago's West Side in November 1934. Law enforcement officers managed to corner feared Dillinger gang member George "Baby Face" Nelson near the city park, and a harrowing car chase ended in a bloodbath that left several dead—and created an enduring mystery about the final hours of the bank robber's life.

"Baby Face" Nelson was born Lester Gillis in Chicago on December 6, 1908. He grew up just steps away from the South Side Stockyards and roamed the streets with a gang of young hoodlums during his early teens. He grew up tough, but at five feet, four inches tall, his height was always a source of agitation. He wanted recognition and fame, and later in life he got both as one of the most bloodthirsty bandits of the Depression era.

By the age of fourteen, Gillis was an accomplished car thief, and while he wanted to be known as "Big George" Nelson, fellow members of his gang dubbed him "Baby Face" because of his juvenile appearance. Nelson's early career included stealing tires, bootlegging and armed robbery. In 1922, he was convicted of auto theft and committed to a boys' home. He was paroled two years later, but within five months he was back in again on another charge. When he was finally released, Nelson graduated from petty theft to sticking up brothels and bookie joints and then selling the same establishments protection against further theft.

While working the protection rackets in 1928, he met a pretty young salesgirl named Helen Wawzynak at a Chicago Woolworth's store, and

The infamous public enemy Lester Gillis, who became better known by his nickname of Baby Face Nelson. *Courtesy of the Library of Congress.*

Nelson met a young Woolworth's salesgirl named Helen Wawzynak in 1928. The two were married and began raising a family. Helen stayed by her husband's side right up until his death. *Courtesy of the Library of Congress.*

he married her. His wife retained the name Helen Gillis throughout their marriage. She stuck with him no matter what happened and stayed with him until the end of his life.

In 1929, Nelson began working for the Capone operation, specializing in labor relations. He could always be counted on to get labor unions to kick back part of their dues to the organization. He enforced his demands with beatings and strong-arm tactics, and eventually his brutality got him dropped from the roster of reliable gunmen. Nelson went back to robberies and, later that year, was apprehended for a jewelry store heist.

Nelson was sent to prison in January 1931 and, after a year's confinement, was removed from the state penitentiary in Joliet to stand trial for a bank robbery charge in Wheaton. On February 17, 1932, he escaped from prison guards while being returned to Joliet and fled the state. He turned up next in Reno, Nevada, and then moved on to Sausalito, California. There, he met John Paul Chase, with whom he would be closely associated for the rest of his life.

Chase, who was just a few years older than Nelson, had lived most of his life in California. He had worked on ranches and in railroad repair shops, and then, in 1930, he became associated with a liquor-smuggling operation run by bootlegger Joe Parente. When Nelson arrived in California, Chase was still involved with the bootleg gang. Nelson worked with Chase as an armed guard for the liquor trucks, and the two of them became close friends. Chase frequently introduced Nelson as his half brother.

Nelson's wife joined him, and they remained in California until May 1933. Nelson went to Long Beach, Indiana, to recruit a bank-robbing gang. The first member of his crew, after Chase, was expert machine-gunner Tommy Carroll, a lighthearted character who had once been a promising boxer. Eddie Green, an expert at scouting out bank locations, also joined Nelson, and they began hitting banks all over the Midwest.

In February 1934, Nelson and the others joined up with the Dillinger gang. By then, most of the members of Dillinger's original gang, save for Homer Van Meter and John Hamilton, had been killed or incarcerated. They worked together during several chaotic and dangerous robberies and then ended up at the Little Bohemia Lodge in Wisconsin in April 1934.

When the FBI agents arrived, the gangsters managed to slip away, leaving wives and girlfriends, including Helen Gillis, behind.

Nelson fled to nearby Sylvan Lodge and forced the elderly owners to take him south on U.S. 51. Their ancient car only made it a few miles before it died near a place belonging to a man named Alvin Koerner.

Nelson pushed his hostages across the road and headed for the lights of the house. Koerner saw him coming, grabbed the telephone and notified the agents at Birchwood Lodge. Nelson broke into the house and added the Koerners to his group of hostages. A few minutes later, several more men arrived, and Nelson commandeered their car. Before he could leave, however, another car arrived carrying FBI agents Jay Newman, Carter Baum and the local constable. They identified themselves as federal agents and asked for Koerner.

Nelson rushed out from behind the other automobile and ordered the agents to get out of the car. A gun was pressed to Newman's head, and he leaned back to give his companions room to fire at Nelson. Unfortunately, they hesitated and Nelson fired first. The first shot grazed Newman's forehead, knocking him back against the seat. Nelson then fired thirteen more times, instantly killing Agent Baum. The constable spilled out the other side of the car and tried to run, but Nelson cut him down. He fired several times at the constable lying in a ditch and then jumped into the car and sped away.

Just down the road, Nelson encountered a carful of incoming agents from St. Paul on U.S. 51. Nelson blinded them with a custom spotlight that had been mounted on the side of the car and then blew past, leading the agents to believe that he was a local police officer. Despite the advantage of the spotlight and the souped-up automobile that he was driving, Nelson didn't make it out of state. The Ford was later found mired in the mud at the mouth of Wisconsin I-55, where the road dead-ended, no doubt to Nelson's surprise, near Star Lake.

The determined gangster walked eighteen miles to the Lac du Flambeau Indian Reservation. He befriended the Schroeders, a family with Native American relatives who were staying in a remote cabin there. The place had no access to radios, telephones or newspapers, and unaware of the raid on Little Bohemia, Mary Schroeder fed the young stranger bacon and eggs, gave him some of her husband's clothes and offered him a cot to sleep on. Nelson paid her $300 and traded his fedora as a souvenir.

Nelson was still there on Monday afternoon when Ollie and Maggie Catfish, Mary Schroeder's aunt and uncle, came to visit. Ollie and his wife, Chippewa Indians, had heard the news but kept silent when they recognized Nelson. The bank robber stayed around until Thursday afternoon, chopping wood and helping with chores. He generously paid Ollie seventy-five dollars for the privilege. Nelson then "rented" (at gunpoint) a 1933 Plymouth from a mail carrier for twenty dollars and took off west toward Wisconsin 70. Ollie Catfish served as his guide, or hostage, to help him avoid any more

The Battle of Barrington

The Lake Como Inn at Lake Geneva, Wisconsin. *Courtesy of the Library of Congress.*

unexpected dead ends. When they reached the highway, Nelson let Ollie out and headed east, searching for a route to Chicago.

Nelson switched cars again in Marshfield, this time buying a 1929 Chevrolet for $165. He continued to Chicago, traveling in and out of Fox River Grove over the next few weeks. He hired a Chicago lawyer to try and spring his wife in Wisconsin, while the couple's children, a five-year-old boy and a four-year-old girl, stayed with Nelson's sister at 5516 Marshfield Avenue in Chicago. The Dillinger girls appeared before a federal magistrate on May 25, and all of them feigned ignorance, offered guilty pleas to harboring fugitives and were let off with a probationary slap on the wrist. Helen joined her husband about a month later.

After Dillinger was killed at the Biograph Theatre in July 1934, Nelson, Helen and John Paul Chase left Chicago for California. That summer, Nelson and Chase made several trips back and forth, and on one occasion, they were stopped for speeding in a small town. They paid the five-dollar fine at the local police station and were released. The automobile, which contained machine guns, rifles and ammunition, was never searched.

In late August, they returned to Chicago, and a month later, Nelson went to Nevada and Chase traveled to New York City. They eventually joined up again in Chicago, and on November 26, they went to Wisconsin.

On November 27, the feds tracked Nelson, Helen and Chase to Wisconsin. The trio intended to hide out at the Lake Como Inn (now the French Country Inn), just north of the Illinois state line. The Lake Como was a no-questions-asked kind of place on the waterfront, owned by Hobart Hermansen, a former bootlegger who was courting the estranged wife of George "Bugs" Moran. Moran had a summer place a little farther down the same dirt road. FBI agents received a tip from Chase's girlfriend, Sally Blackman, that the bank robbers intended to winter at the inn. The agents pressured Hermansen into loaning them his place. They were caught off guard when a Ford they mistook for the owner's pulled up out front. Nelson realized that he had driven into an ambush at the same time the agents recognized the driver of the car. Nelson, with a pistol hidden on his lap, exchanged a few pleasantries with the agents and then drove away unhindered, since one of the agents had driven the only FBI auto into the nearby town of Lake Geneva for groceries.

A frantic telephone call to Chicago sent three carloads of federal agents toward Wisconsin in hopes of intercepting Nelson on the Northwest Highway (then U.S. 12, now U.S. 14). The first team of agents, Thomas McDade and William Ryan, encountered Nelson's car near the village of Fox River Grove and turned around to chase him, only to discover that Nelson had also turned around. As the two vehicles passed one another a second time, Nelson spun the wheel and, instead of running, started chasing his pursuers. The surprised feds accelerated, but Nelson stayed right behind them. Agent McDade pressed the gas pedal to the floor, and his car surged ahead. As he did so, Nelson grabbed Helen's shoulder, pushed her down to the floor of the car and screamed at Chase to let them have it.

Chase opened fire, and his bullets punched holes in the right side of the agents' windshield. Nelson accelerated to keep pace with the FBI men, snatched up his pistol with his left hand, leaned it out the window and began firing shots at the car ahead. Agent Ryan returned fire, blasting out the back window of Nelson's car. He fired a full clip at the pursuing sedan. Meanwhile, McDade struggled to keep control of the car, which was now traveling at more than seventy-five miles per hour. They were rapidly overtaking a slow-moving milk truck lumbering along in the lane ahead of them.

As Ryan's automatic emptied, he reached for a second pistol and realized that Nelson's car had backed off. He told McDade, who had not had time to worry about the gangsters behind them. McDade swerved into the opposite lane to miss the milk truck and was horrified to see a westbound car hurtling toward them. He pushed the car ahead and managed to pass the truck and swerve back into the right lane, narrowly avoiding a fatal collision.

Ryan continued to watch through the ragged glass of the back window as he saw Nelson maneuver around the milk truck and then slow down to widen the gap between them. Suddenly, McDade missed a sharp turn in the road, and the car bounced into a field and came to a stop. Both agents jumped out, guns in hand, and took cover behind the vehicle. However, Nelson's sedan never appeared.

Ryan and McDade were not aware that within moments of pulling away from Nelson, two more FBI agents had joined the chase, once again turning Nelson into the one being pursued. At some point between Fox River Grove and Barrington, agents Sam Cowley and Herman Hollis encountered the high-speed gun battle that was taking place. Wondering why it was going in the wrong direction with the wrong car in pursuit, they turned around to try and catch up with Nelson from behind.

As they came up behind Nelson's Ford, they saw smoke and steam start to billow from under the hood. Apparently, a bullet from Ryan's gun had struck the radiator of Nelson's car. As the gangster hopelessly punched the accelerator, the second FBI car came in close behind. One of the agents leaned out the window of the car with a machine gun in his hand. As Chase opened fire, Nelson tried valiantly to get just a little more speed and distance from the faltering car. The guns roared as Helen crouched on the floor, her head between her knees and her left hand clutching her husband's leg.

Through the smoke that was churning from the damaged engine, Nelson saw that they were entering the northwest side of Barrington. The FBI car continued to gain on them and then pulled alongside. Nelson had to make a desperate move.

Ahead, along the north side of the highway, were three gas stations—a Standard, a Shell and a Sinclair. On the opposite side of the highway, surrounded by mostly open field, was a gravel road leading to Barrington's North Side Park. About four hundred yards ahead, houses began to appear on both sides of the road.

Thinking fast, Nelson suddenly swerved into the park entrance and hit the brakes, causing the Ford to slide to a stop. Hollis slammed on his brakes, but the FBI vehicle skidded past the entrance in a long, shaking slide. As the car passed by Nelson's halted automobile, Agent Cowley fired a burst of shots.

Nelson ordered the others out of the vehicle and lunged out the driver's side door. He hurried around to the back of the car as Chase and his wife tumbled out of the passenger's side. He yelled at his wife to run, instructing her to get into the nearby field and lay flat on the ground. Helen sprinted through the tall grass between the road and the park's football field, dropping to her stomach as gunfire erupted.

The first shots came from Chase, who was crouched at the front of the Ford. Steam from the damaged radiator slightly concealed his position, and he used the distraction to open up on the FBI agents on the road. Seconds later, Nelson, standing at the rear of the sedan with a machine gun, also opened fire.

The FBI agent's Hudson had screeched to a halt in the middle of the highway, about 120 feet away. Bullets tore into the vehicle as Cowley jumped out of the passenger side and took cover behind the vehicle. Hollis, shotgun in hand, scrambled out of the same door and hid behind the front bumper. For the next three minutes, a furious battle raged as bullets slammed into the two cars, kicked up clouds of dust and bounced off the pavement.

Hidden in the weeds about twenty yards from the Ford, Helen raised her head for one quick look as the shooting continued. She later reported, "I saw Les jump and grab his side. I knew then that was the end."

Less than a minute into the battle, a .45 slug from Cowley's Thompson machine gun pierced Nelson's left side, just above his belt. The bullet tore through his liver and pancreas before punching a hole out of the lower-right portion of his back. Doubled over and clasping his side, he ran to the running board of the car and exchanged weapons with Chase, firing the other bandit's gun as Chase reloaded his own. No words were spoken, according to Chase, who later swore that he didn't know his friend had been wounded.

With a fresh drum in his Thompson, Nelson attempted to fire through the Ford's side window. Between shots, Chase heard him complain about his weapon jamming, and he threw it aside. Nelson picked up a rifle from the backseat and moved to the rear of the vehicle. Chase assumed that he was going back to his original position but soon discovered that Nelson had walked out into the open and was advancing on the FBI agents and their Hudson.

Nelson charged at them, almost manically, firing and sweeping his weapon back and forth. Cowley suddenly abandoned his position and darted left to the south side of the highway, where he stumbled into the ditch. Rising to his knees, he attempted to shoot at Nelson, but his machine gun refused to fire. Nelson sent several slugs in his direction, and Cowley crumpled onto his left side.

A second later, Hollis leaned out and fired his shotgun. The impact from the heavy weapon knocked the legs out from under Nelson. He fell to the ground but managed get back up and kept on coming toward the FBI agent.

Nelson fired at Hollis, turned to fire several more shots at the downed Cowley and then hammered the front of the Hudson.

As Nelson came closer, Hollis turned and tried to run. He ran toward a telephone pole on the north side of the road, located between the Standard and Shell stations. As he ran, he fired backward at Nelson, but then his gun jammed. As he neared the telephone pole, he dropped the shotgun and drew an automatic from inside his coat. Before he could fire, Nelson's next barrage of bullets hit him. Nelson kept coming at the agent, firing again and again as Hollis slumped against the wooden pole, which was now chewed up by stray bullets. He cried out and then fell facedown onto the edge of the highway.

Nelson stood over the agent for a moment, his weapon poised to fire more shots into the man on the ground, but then he lowered it, apparently satisfied that Hollis was dead. He limped across the road toward the Hudson, dragging his left leg behind him and spattering blood on the pavement. He climbed behind the wheel of the Hudson and pulled up behind the disabled Ford. He shouted for Helen and Chase, who gathered their weapons and trotted over to where Nelson was parked in the car. When he saw Chase, Nelson groaned, "Drop everything and get me to a priest."

Chase told him to wait a minute while he grabbed their cases from the other car, but Nelson told him to forget all of it. He tried to crawl over the passenger side, leaving a trail of gore on the seat. He told Chase, "You'll have to drive, I'm hit pretty hard."

Helen came running out of the field and climbed into the car. Chase hit the accelerator, pointing the vehicle back west toward Fox River Grove. Helen sat in the back, next to her wounded husband, cradling his head in her arms. Nelson looked up at her, his eyes blurry and filled with pain. "I'm done for," he gasped.

Chase drove as fast as he could along the unfamiliar road, with no idea where to go. Nelson was slumped against the passenger door, drawing deep breaths, while Helen wept and continued to hold his sagging body. Nelson did the best he could to direct his friend to safety. Three miles west of Barrington, he told him to turn right on Kelsey Road and then right again on Route 22. Driving east, they passed two miles north of Barrington, heading toward Lake Zurich. When not in town, Chase kept the gas pedal mashed to the floor, and within a half hour they reached Highland Park. Nelson was fading fast, but he instructed Chase to head south on Skokie Road. Entering Wilmette, they drove to 1155 Mohawk Road, a home that belonged to the sister of Father Phillip Coughlan, a Catholic priest who had

The sedan used by Nelson and Chase during the Battle of Barrington attracted a large crowd of spectators. The man in the photo points to holes punched in the windshield by Chase, who was firing a rifle from the backseat at fleeing FBI agents. *Courtesy of the Library of Congress.*

grown up on Chicago's West Side and had close ties to many gangsters and underworld figures.

Late in the afternoon, the rectory maid notified Father Coughlan that there was a young woman knocking on the back-door window, asking to see him. The priest went to the kitchen and found Helen Gillis in the doorway. She told him that her husband had been shot and needed his help. Coughlan grabbed his coat and hat and followed her. Chase had pulled into the garage and helped Nelson get out, hoping to bring his wounded friend into the house. Nelson muttered a faint greeting when the priest arrived. He was leaning against the back of the car, his face white and bloodless. Helen begged the priest to bring Nelson inside, but Coughlan refused because it was his sister's house. Instead, he offered to lead them to a safe location. Helen asked that they all go in the same car, but again, the priest refused. The bullet-riddled Hudson could not remain in his sister's garage. Coughlan helped to ease Nelson back into the passenger's seat of the Hudson. Once the bandit was situated, the priest noticed a warm stickiness on his right hand. He looked down to see that it was covered with blood.

Father Coughlan got into his Ford coupe and backed out into the street. With the Hudson following, he turned north on Ashland Avenue and then west on Skokie Road. Two blocks later, he noticed the Hudson do a quick

U-turn and speed off in the opposite direction. He turned around and tried to catch up with them, but he lost the vehicle in traffic near Lake Street. He later confessed that he was relieved but also saddened. He realized that Nelson must have thought he was leading them into a trap.

Coughlan was right. Even in his weakened state, Nelson was suspicious about the way the priest was acting, mistaking his confusion about where to safely hide the injured outlaw for possible betrayal. As they drove, he instructed Chase to lose him, and they headed off with an alternate destination in mind. Nelson feebly told Chase where and when to turn, traveling south and keeping mostly to residential streets as they left Wilmette and entered Winnetka, then Niles Center (now Skokie). At one point, Nelson appeared to pass out, and Chase turned into an alley to wait for him to wake up. A minute or so later, Nelson regained consciousness and urged his friend to keep driving.

On Sixteenth Street, Nelson told Chase to slow down. Pointing to a narrow alley that ran behind Walnut Street, he told him to make the turn. Chase drove down the alley to a red two-car garage at the rear of a light gray stucco cottage that faced Walnut Street. The address of the cottage was 1627 Walnut Street. Chase pulled into the garage and asked Nelson who lived there. Nelson mumbled, "Friends."

Chase went to the front door and knocked. A tall, dark-complexioned man in his late thirties answered. Chase told him that someone outside needed him, and the man accompanied him to the garage. When the man saw Nelson in the car, Chase knew that he instantly recognized him. The two men, with Helen following, carried Nelson into the house. They entered through a side door and passed through the kitchen. Along the way, Chase glimpsed an older man and a young woman who appeared frightened at the sight of the bloody and wounded bandit. They went into a small bedroom, where they placed Nelson on a large iron bed. The other man walked out, leaving Chase and Helen to take care of Nelson. Helen later recounted, "All three of us knew Les was dying, but there was nothing we could do."

They did their best to make him comfortable and stop the bleeding. Helen was given scissors and other supplies, and she cut the bloody clothing from her husband's body. She stuffed cotton into the bullet hole in his stomach and the gaping exit wound in his back, and then covered both wounds by wrapping him with long strips of cloth torn from a bedsheet. Helen cleaned his buckshot-spattered legs and covered him with a blanket when he told her that he was cold.

Nelson sighed. He felt better, he told his wife and friends. The pain was gone, and now he just felt numb all over. Helen held his hand and waited for the end to come.

About an hour after Nelson, Helen and Chase arrived at the house on Walnut Street, the man who had helped carry the bank robber inside came and told Chase that he needed to move the damaged government vehicle. Chase agreed, but Nelson begged him not to leave. Minutes later, the man came back and reiterated that the car had to be moved. Nelson again appealed to his friend to stay, and Chase promised he would, but noticing that Nelson was slipping in and out of consciousness, he made the decision to slip away for a few minutes. Before long, Chase quietly left the bedside, exited through the side door and drove away. He later insisted that he had planned to return after he ditched the car, but being unfamiliar with the area, he soon became lost. Attempting to head south into Chicago, he ended up going north and found himself back in Winnetka. When the Hudson ran out of gas, he abandoned it near some railroad tracks. This forced him to make another decision. Knowing that there was nothing he could do to help his friend, he realized that he needed to try to get away. Chase caught a train to Chicago and disappeared.

Helen was left alone with her dying husband. Shortly after Chase departed, Nelson seemed to realize that he had little time left. He asked Helen to say goodbye to their family, and when he began to talk about their children, he cried a little. Finally, he gasped out his final words, "It's getting dark, Helen. I can't see you anymore."

Nelson's eyes glazed over. His breathing became shallow and raspy and then stopped altogether. The infamous Baby Face Nelson was dead.

Rain fell on the Walnut Street cottage until the early morning hours. Helen Gillis sat with her husband's corpse until nearly dawn, and then the man who had helped them came into the room and told her that the body needed to be moved. Helen wanted to take her husband to an undertaker's, but she knew that was impossible. The man told her that he would find a place where the body could be left. He promised to call an undertaker later on.

After wrapping the body in an imitation Indian blanket, Helen and the man carried it outside and placed it in the backseat of an Oldsmobile that was parked in the driveway. Helen climbed in next to her husband, cradling him in her arms as the man drove. They drove deeper into Niles Center, and at the southwest corner of Niles (now Conrad) and Long Avenues, they reached St. Paul's Cemetery. The driver pulled over to the curb, and they wrestled the body from the car. Nelson's naked, bloody corpse was placed on the grass. Helen tucked the blanket around him, hoping that he would be comfortable because Lester "always hated the cold."

A few blocks away, just south of Howard Avenue, Helen dropped Nelson's bloodstained clothing out the window. The driver continued south until they reached Chicago's North Side. The man asked her if this was a suitable spot for her to be let out, and she said that it was, even though she had no idea where she was or where she should go. Before she stepped out of the car, she gave the driver the name of a mortician who had handled the funerals of her mother and her sister. He promised to call and notify the undertaker where to find Nelson's body, and then he drove away.

Helen wandered the unfamiliar streets for over an hour. Finally, at about 5:00 a.m., she hailed a cab and slipped into the warm backseat. The driver asked her where she wanted to go, and she told him to just keep driving.

At 6:45 a.m. the bullet-riddled Hudson was discovered by a Winnetka milkman, who notified a local patrolman. Federal agents arrived at the scene within an hour and found bullet holes and plenty of blood.

At 7:30 a.m., Philip Sadowski, the owner of a funeral home on North Hermitage Avenue, received a telephone call from a man with a "rough voice" who informed him that the body of a man named Gillis was lying in a graveyard in Niles Center, a block away from Harms Road. Sadowski told the man that he was unable to retrieve the body. He was in the midst of preparing for a funeral, and besides, he added, morticians don't recover bodies. The man would have to notify the coroner to do that. The man on the other end of the line told Sadowski to notify anyone he wanted to but to handle the arrangements.

Sadowski reported the anonymous call to the Chicago Coroner's Office and was advised to contact the Niles Center Police. Acting on the undertaker's information, Captain Axel Stolberg and a patrolman went out to the area to look around. Sadowski, however, had failed to mention the name of the cemetery, and the body was not found. The pair returned to the police station, only to hear about a call that had just come in from someone who found bloody clothing near where the officers had been searching.

News of the discovery was passed on to federal agents, who had spent the morning searching Winnetka. Four agents arrived to help Captain Stolberg search the area again. It was almost noon when FBI agent Sam McKee signaled that he had found the remains of Baby Face Nelson.

Nelson's body lay in the grass, with his head resting on the curb. He was naked, except for the cloth strips that had been wrapped about his waist, and he was drenched in blood. His right arm was across his chest and his left hand was frozen into a claw just above the wound in his stomach. His feet were crossed, and the agents realized that he had been dead long enough for rigor mortis to set in. The body was picked up, carried to a car and driven to the mortuary for an official identification. Fingerprints confirmed that the dead man was Lester Gillis, aka Baby Face Nelson.

The body was photographed and examined. The press reported that Nelson had been shot seventeen times, but the official count was actually nine. By midafternoon, news of Nelson's death was sweeping the city. The body was transported to the Cook County Morgue and placed on a slab for public display. More than two thousand morbid curiosity-seekers filed past the dead bank robber in the hours that followed.

Once Nelson was confirmed dead, the massive manhunt for the killers of FBI agents Cowley and Hollis shifted to his two companions at the Battle of Barrington—John Chase and Helen Gillis.

With little cash and no car, Chase had checked into the Garfield Arms, a downtown hotel, and hid out in his room, only venturing out a couple of times to buy newspapers. Chase soon devised a clever way to get out of the city by answering a newspaper ad looking for drivers to deliver automobiles to the West Coast. Using the name Elmer Rockwood, Chase applied and

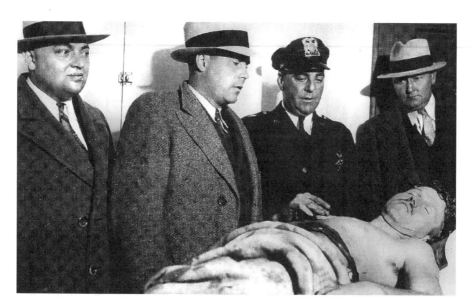

Police officers and FBI agents were anxious to be photographed with the body of Baby Face Nelson, America's public enemy number one. *Courtesy of the Library of Congress.*

was accepted. He received a paycheck for driving a Studebaker to Seattle, and when he arrived there, he disappeared again.

The search for Helen drew the most publicity. When Hoover ordered his agents to "find the woman and give her no quarter," the press interpreted this to mean that Helen was to be shot on sight. Some stories even suggested that she had replaced her husband as public enemy number one. Even worse, a United Press story labeled Helen "the Tiger Woman" and portrayed her as a "ruthless gun moll of the Bonnie Parker type, leading her cohorts in bank raids and battles with officers of the law." She was the brains of the gang, it claimed, pushing her husband into a life of crime. The account also claimed that during the gunfight in Barrington, Helen had been loading guns for Nelson and Chase.

Of course, nothing could be further from the truth, but even the FBI started to believe the newspapers. One agent was quoted as saying, "I'd hate to shoot a woman but I'm not following Cowley and Hollis because of ideas over a woman like that." Assistant Director Clegg echoed the sentiments when reporters asked him what the government's procedures were for apprehending Helen. He told the newsmen, "From now on, mercy goes by the boards."

On Thanksgiving morning, November 29, Helen Gillis—America's most wanted "outlaw" and the so-called "Tiger Woman"—resumed wandering the streets of Chicago. She had spent most of the night sleeping in the doorway of an abandoned building. She eventually ended up in her old neighborhood, where she watched her father, from a safe distance, as he left for work with a small crowd of people around him. The ones who were not reporters were FBI agents, waiting for Helen to show up. Asked if he had a statement for his daughter, Vincent Warwick made a plea that was published the following day: "Come home. Surrender and give up alive or you'll be mowed down by machine guns. Remember your babies."

Helen moved on and spent the rest of the day around Humboldt Park. She considered calling her sister-in-law, Julie, but was certain that her telephone was tapped. As evening approached, she dreaded the idea of spending another night on the streets. Near Lafayette School, she stopped a young girl and paid her a dollar to deliver a note to Julie's apartment.

At that moment, Julie's husband, Bob Fitzsimmons, was on the phone, as he had been most of the day. This time, he was speaking with Special Agent McKee, who had called to ask about the time and place of Nelson's funeral. According to Helen's wishes, the body had been turned over to Sadowski's funeral home, but no arrangements had been made. McKee urged Fitzsimmons to try and get Helen to turn herself in. Bob agreed to do his best to get the family to contact her. If they were successful, he asked that agents take her into custody in a quiet manner, avoiding publicity if possible.

Just minutes after Fitzsimmons hung up, the girl arrived with Helen's note. Bob and Julie immediately left the house, and when they were certain they were not being followed, they went to the school and found Helen sitting in the dark on the front steps. For the next hour, they drove around as Helen tearfully told them everything that had taken place. She said that she would have surrendered sooner but she was afraid that she might be shot. She added that she was hopeful that a deal could be arranged with the FBI that would allow her to attend her husband's funeral.

At 10:25 p.m., Fitzsimmons called the FBI and was put in touch with Special Agent Virgil Peterson. He passed on the wish that Helen wanted to surrender but also asked if she could be allowed to attend her husband's funeral. Peterson was in no mood to bargain. He told Bob that no promises could be made and demanded that Helen immediately turn herself in. It would be in her best interests, he emphasized, if she surrendered. After Helen agreed, Fitzsimmons told him that they would meet the FBI agents at the southwest corner of Jackson Boulevard and Halsted Street.

A short time later, Helen was taken into custody. The press was not notified of the arrangement. At the Banker's Building, Helen was surrounded by six agents and hurried into the building through a rear entrance. After checking to be sure that no newsmen were present, she was taken to the nineteenth floor, led along a little-used passage that cut through a storage room and placed in the main office.

For the next five days, Helen's presence in the building was kept secret while she was interrogated by the federal men. Hoover stressed that she must be made to talk and that Earl Connelly, who had stepped into the role of head of the Chicago office after Hoover had moved out Melvin Purvis, should question her constantly so that she would be unable to sleep. But Connelly was not cruel. In fact, Helen later stated that he was very nice and treated her quite well.

Helen did talk, however. She reluctantly shared an abundance of information while carefully avoiding the mention of any crucial names. Many of Nelson's associates were merely "friends of Les," whose names she claimed she didn't know or couldn't recall. Their companion at Barrington, Helen said, was "a fellow named George."

Helen spoke of her entire history with Nelson, but agents were most interested in the gangster's final hours. They were determined to know where he had gone to die and who had helped him in his final hours.

Helen was evasive at first, insisting that Les had been conscious and had directed "George" during the entire trip. Nelson guided them to a house that she had never been to before, but she described it when pressed for details. Finally, she was taken in a car and forced to lead them, block by block and turn by turn, to Wilmette and eventually to Walnut Street. The bungalow she took them to was just as she had described it in the FBI office.

An immediate and rather extensive investigation was started. With the cooperation of neighbors, FBI agents began around-the-clock surveillance of the cottage at 1627 Walnut Street. Over the next several weeks, the agents noted the comings and goings of the occupants and their visitors. They spoke to neighbors, checked license numbers, consulted public records and even got the local postman involved. According to what they learned, the occupants of the house were Raymond J. Henderson, an unemployed truck driver who was currently receiving relief checks; his wife, Marie; a son, age fourteen; and a daughter, age twelve. The Hendersons had a questionable reputation with the local police, but this was not the most interesting discovery the agents made.

According to the postman, several different individuals used the mailing address of the house and, from time to time, actually lived there. The part-time residents included Guy McDonald, a known hood and one-time business associate of former mail-train robber Jimmy Murray. McDonald often vanished and then returned to the house, and lately, he had been around again. He was often seen at the house, and neighborhood gossip claimed that Mrs. Henderson was heard bragging about the fact that she was sleeping with McDonald.

The Hendersons and their houseguests were eventually brought in and questioned, and all of them adamantly denied knowing Nelson and swore that he had not come to their house on the day of his death or at any other time. With that, the FBI probe into the house at 1627 Walnut Street unexpectedly ended. The fact that no arrests were made and no charges filed was likely because of lack of evidence. But this hardly explains the abrupt closing of the case, especially since Hoover's direct orders to the agents in Chicago were to uncover the identities of everyone involved and have them prosecuted.

Today, the circumstances surrounding Nelson's death, and exactly who was present, remain an intriguing and unsolved mystery. Few details were reported in the usually obsessive press, and the FBI never publicly revealed where Nelson died or charged those who offered him shelter. Bureau files still remain strangely silent concerning the investigation that took place.

The only clue in this seemingly odd decision not to prosecute was found in a document that was filed four years later, in 1937. It contained a statement from a neighbor, who told FBI agents that the woman still living in the house said it belonged to someone closely connected with the FBI, probably as an informant. This individual had also been supplying Nelson with inside information about the movements of law enforcement officials. Nelson, the neighbor said, had decided the Walnut Street house would be the last place that federal agents would think to look for him—hiding with one of their own.

Although the amount of information offered in the report is limited, it does allow speculation that the FBI, upon discovering where Nelson died, decided to let the matter go rather than reveal that he had spent his last hours in the care of someone connected with the FBI. Public disclosure would have proven embarrassing, so the whole thing was covered up. Who the informant may have been remains unknown to this day. The person's identity, and his or her relationship with the FBI, was concealed by blotting out the name on the existing records.

No further information ever appeared, and either the investigating agents never wanted to solve the mystery of Nelson's death or they already knew what happened.

On December 4, word finally leaked to the press that Helen Gillis had been in federal custody since Thanksgiving night. No details were given about her surrender, only that she had been "cooperating" under questioning. The bureau wanted to hold her longer for further interrogation, but once word got out, it was forced to proceed with the only legal recourse available.

On December 6, Helen was delivered to the Dane County Jail in Madison, Wisconsin, where she had been taken after the raid on Little Bohemia. The next morning, she was brought to the judge's chambers, and he asked her why she had violated her probation. She could only tell him, "I knew Les didn't have long to live, and I wanted to be with him as long as I could."

More than 150 spectators jammed the courtroom for her hearing. Looking small and frail, Helen admitted that she had violated her probation. Her probation was revoked, and she was taken immediately to serve her sentence of a year and a day at the Women's Correctional Farm at Milan, Michigan.

The Battle of Barrington

In December, the authorities were still looking for John Chase. On December 26, he hitchhiked to Mount Shasta and visited a fish hatchery, where he had worked five years before. He told a foreman that he was broke and borrowed a few dollars. That same foreman called the police after Chase left and said that the fugitive had stated that he was staying at the Park Hotel. When Police Chief Al Roberts and a deputy sheriff arrived at the hotel, they discovered that their suspect had just left. A few blocks away, they spotted Chase walking along the street and quietly arrested him.

Chase was turned over to federal agents, who took him to San Francisco for several days of questioning. He admitted that he had been Nelson's friend and had traveled with him for nearly a year, but he denied taking part in any bank robberies or gun fights—except for the Battle of Barrington, in which he insisted he had only fired in self-defense and had not been responsible for the murder of either of the federal agents.

Chase was taken by train to Chicago on New Year's Eve, where he was the first person to be tried under the law that made it a federal violation to murder a special agent of the FBI in the performance of his duties. Chase's trial began on March 18, 1935. One week later, the jury found him guilty of murdering Sam Cowley but recommended leniency. He was sentenced to life imprisonment on Alcatraz.

Chase was a model prisoner on "the Rock," well liked by other inmates and the staff. During his time there, the only hint of trouble occurred in 1937, when prison officials suspected him of conspiring with two inmates who attempted to escape. As it turned out, the inmates had befriended Chase to take advantage of his knowledge of the Bay Area. Chase was happy to give them information, but he never planned to take part in the escape.

Over the years, he developed a passion for painting and was regarded by many as an accomplished artist. He also became close friends with the prison chaplain, who obtained painting materials for Chase by selling some of his work in San Francisco.

In 1955, Chase became eligible for parole, and the chaplain became his strongest advocate, insisting that Chase was a changed man who could be a useful part of society. J. Edgar Hoover heard of the chaplain's campaign on Chase's behalf and immediately started to work against him, ensuring that Chase remained on Alcatraz. At the bottom of a memo, Hoover wrote, "Watch closely and endeavor to thwart efforts of this priest who should be attending to his own business instead of trying to turn loose on society such mad dogs."

Two years later, Hoover was stunned to learn that one of his former agents had supported Chase's parole. Tom McDade, one of the men who had been shot at by Chase on the Northwest Highway, wrote to the Alcatraz chaplain saying that he had no objection to Chase's release. Hoover branded McDade, who was already retired, a traitor to the bureau.

In September 1954, Chase was transferred to Leavenworth, and seven months later, he received his first parole hearing. He discovered that federal prosecutors, prodded by Hoover, were ready to indict him for the murder of Herman Hollis if he were set free. Hoover had used FBI agents to track down a dozen witnesses against Chase, including a feeble Father Coughlan, who was living out his final days in a retirement home in Jasper, Indiana. Chase filed a petition in federal court charging that the government had intentionally withheld the twenty-two-year-old murder charge in order to block his application for parole at this time. A judge ruled to dismiss the indictment, stating that the idea of prosecuting a man on a charge that had been gathering dust for two decades "shocks the imagination and the conscience."

In spite of the federal judge's statements, Hoover continued to write letters and make calls to the parole board in protest. Finally, on October 31, 1966, Chase was released. He moved to Palo Alto, California, where he lived a quiet life, working as a custodian and performing odd jobs until his death in October 1973 from colon cancer.

Despite being a model prisoner while behind bars, Helen Gillis served almost the entire year of her sentence. On December 6, 1935, federal agents escorted her to San Francisco, where she was arraigned on charges of harboring her late husband and placed in a cell to await trial.

Assistant U.S. Attorney R.B. McMillan, who was supposed to prosecute Helen, wrote a letter to the attorney general stating that the twenty-two-year-old widow was clearly no threat to society and appeared so pathetic that further prosecution seemed pointless. Hoover received a copy of the letter and was enraged. He insisted that the wife of Baby Face Nelson belonged in prison.

Helen appeared in court on December 13. The young woman who had married Lester Gillis seven years earlier, and who had been the constant companion of Baby Face Nelson, quietly pleaded guilty and applied for probation. Her attorney stated that she was only guilty of being a faithful wife to a misguided husband, adding that she had been punished enough.

Prosecutor McMillan (likely to Hoover's chagrin) added his recommendation to her plea for probation, citing her record of excellent behavior over her past year in federal custody. Finally, the judge declared, "I believe you've been punished enough. I want you to lead a good life and be a good mother to your children."

Helen was ordered to serve one year's probation and, finally, was free.

She gave very few interviews in the years that followed, but on one occasion, she summed up her life with Nelson. "I loved Les. When you love a guy, you love him. That's all there is to it. If I had my life to live over again, I'd do just as I did. I'd stick to my husband any time, any place, no matter what he did."

Helen grieved, and then she got on with her life. In 1937, she returned to Chicago with her children and spent the next fifty years staying away from publicity. Her children married and moved away—Ronald to LaFox, Illinois, and Darlene to southern Wisconsin. Helen visited them frequently, and in her last years, she lived with Ronald.

She never remarried. She died on July 3, 1987, at a hospital in St. Charles, one week after suffering a cerebral hemorrhage. Her last wish was to be buried next to her husband in the Gillis family plot at St. Joseph's Cemetery in River Grove.

On that day, a chapter was closed on a piece of public enemy history as the final participant in the Battle of Barrington was forever laid to rest.

THE MURDER OF EDDIE O'HARE

A number of mysteries still surround the ambush murder of Edward Joseph O'Hare on Chicago's West Side on November 8, 1939. But one thing is certain: his assassination was revenge for crossing Al Capone.

O'Hare was born and raised in the tough Kerry-Patch neighborhood of St. Louis and lucked into a fortune through dog racing. The mechanical rabbit for dog racing was invented by St. Louis promoter Oliver P. Smith. Smith first tested the device with greyhounds in 1909 and spent the next decade developing it. After he filed for a patent, he formed a partnership with a sharp young St. Louis attorney named Eddie O'Hare. For the right to install a mechanical rabbit dog track, the owners paid Smith and O'Hare a percentage of the gate. Smith died in 1927, and under an arrangement with his widow, O'Hare obtained the patent rights for the metal rabbit. He became a major player in the racing world and an overnight millionaire.

O'Hare started his own dog track in Madison, Illinois, across the river from St. Louis, and founded the Madison Kennel Club. The money poured in until a series of police raids forced him to shut down. A Cook County judge, Harry Fisher, meanwhile, had come to the aid of the Capone Outfit by declaring dog tracks legal and preventing the police from raiding them. The judge's brother, Louis Fisher, was the lawyer representing the dog track owners. The Illinois Surpreme Court eventually overruled him, but for a time, Capone prospered with the Hawthorne Kennel Club, located on the outskirts of Cicero.

Arriving in Chicago in the 1920s, O'Hare opened the Lawndale Kennel Club and was set to make a fortune. His track was uncomfortably close to Capone's, but O'Hare had something that everyone else wanted—the mechanical rabbit. He let it be known that should anyone attempt to harm him or put him out of business, he would withhold the rights to the rabbit in Cook County. If he couldn't operate there, no one could.

Capone knew that O'Hare was making huge profits and was not obligated to pay a percentage of the gate for the use of the rabbit. He didn't want to put O'Hare out of business, but he did decide to cut himself into the profits. When he suggested that O'Hare merge his Lawndale Kennel Club with Capone's Hawthorne Kennel Club, O'Hare readily agreed.

Unlike the later closely supervised legal sport, the dog racing of the 1920s was easy to fix, much to the dismay of innocent bettors. For example, if eight greyhounds were run, seven of them could be overfed or run an additional mile before the race, leaving the eighth dog as the almost guaranteed winner.

O'Hare despised the men with whom he had to work almost as much as he loved the money that he was making. But he believed that there was money to be made working with mobsters, as long as he didn't associate with them personally and kept all of his dealings professional.

O'Hare had his own brushes with the law in his past. At the outset of Prohibition, the authorities permitted a liquor wholesaler named George Remus to store about $200,000 worth of whiskey in the same building where O'Hare had his law office. Remus had to put up a $100,000 bond as surety that he would not remove a single bottle without government sanction. Nevertheless, by 1923, all of the liquor had found its way into the bootleg markets of Chicago, New York and other cities, even though Remus never saw a cent of profit. Enraged, he filed charges and caused indictments to be filed against twenty-two men, including Eddie O'Hare. The lawyer was sentenced to a year in jail and fined $500, but he won a reversal on appeal when Remus withdrew his original testimony. O'Hare, it was learned later, offered to pay off Remus to drop the charges against him.

O'Hare quickly made a name for himself in Chicago and earned the nickname of "Artful Eddie." He was a well-mannered, cultivated and handsome man. A strong athlete, he rode, boxed, swam and played golf. He never smoked and never drank hard liquor. Married young, he fathered two girls and a boy. His son, Edward H. O'Hare, nicknamed "Butch," was twelve when his father first met Al Capone. O'Hare idolized the boy, and more than anything that he wanted for himself, he wanted a great career and wonderful life for his son.

O'Hare made many friends in high places. His association with Judge Eugene J. Holland of the Rackets Courts managed to keep more than twelve thousand defendants from serving serious prison time. Holland dismissed all but twenty-eight of those arrested and charged with violations of gambling statutes. O'Hare gained a reputation as a well-connected man to know.

Meanwhile, he was making a fortune with the dog racing track. The public was mad about the sport, and grandstands could not be constructed quickly enough to deal with the increasing crowds. The weekly net ran as high as $50,000. O'Hare acted as both manager and counsel, a double function that he handled with such skill that the syndicate later entrusted him with other dog tracks in Florida and Massachusetts. O'Hare had planned to keep himself socially above Capone and his mobsters, but he became hopelessly entangled in their affairs.

Unbeknownst to his mob friends, Eddie O'Hare became a secret government informant. For nearly eight years, he funneled information about Capone to Internal Revenue Service agent Frank J. Wilson, who had been working to build a tax evasion case against the mobster. A mutual friend, John Rogers of the *St. Louis Post-Dispatch* newspaper, had brought the two men together. They first met over lunch at the Missouri Athletic Club so that O'Hare could look the government agent over and decide if he was really the man to get Capone. "He's satisfied," Rogers told Wilson after the meeting.

O'Hare decided to inform against Capone for paternal reasons. His son, Butch, was determined to attend the U.S. Naval Academy at Annapolis, and O'Hare wanted to smooth the way for him by helping the government bring down Capone and his organization. "If O'Hare had ten lives," John Rogers later said, "he would gladly risk them all for the boy."

Wilson heard from O'Hare frequently after that, either directly or through Rogers. It was O'Hare who told him about the structure of the Capone dog track management and verified that more than half of the profits went directly into Capone's pockets. He also called Wilson one morning to warn him that Capone, acting against the judgment of cooler heads, had brought in five gunmen from New York with a contract to kill Wilson. The contract called for a payment of $25,000, O'Hare told him, and the killers were driving a blue Chevrolet sedan with New York plates. Wilson heeded O'Hare's warning, and he and his wife immediately moved to another hotel. They told the desk clerks at the Sheridan Plaza that they were going to Kansas City, drove to Union Station and then

Federal agent Frank Wilson received all of O'Hare's inside information about the financial dealings of Capone and the Chicago Outfit. O'Hare's tips even managed to save Wilson's life after Capone hired a hit squad to take him out. *Courtesy of the Library of Congress.*

Eddie "Butch" O'Hare, son of dog racing entrepreneur Eddie J. O'Hare and the American hero for whom the O'Hare International Airport is named.

circled back and took a room at the Palmer House. A twenty-four-hour guard was assigned to look after them.

Capone went to prison, but O'Hare's undercover activity didn't end with the Capone case. Despite his long and profitable association with gangsters, O'Hare had detested them from the start. He went on informing against them to both county and state police, undaunted by Wilson's warning that some policeman in the pay of mobsters would betray him. Wilson was right—O'Hare's secret would not remain hidden for long.

Ensign Henry "Butch" O'Hare graduated from Annapolis in 1937 and was sent overseas just after the attack on Pearl Harbor, which marked the United States' entry into World War II. On February 20, 1942, he singlehandedly saved the U.S. Navy carrier *Lexington* from certain destruction. The lone pilot attacked a wing of Japanese fighters, and wreaking havoc on the enemy craft, he prevented an aerial bombardment of the fleet. For his bravery, President Franklin Delano Roosevelt awarded him the Congressional Medal of Honor. More than a year later, in November 1943, Butch O'Hare vanished near Tarawa Island while establishing night radar flights. His body and plane were never found. On September 18, 1949, Orchard Depot, an isolated airfield on the far Northwest Side of Chicago, was formally dedicated O'Hare Field in honor of the brave fighter pilot.

Unfortunately, the hero's father never lived to see the recognition that was given to his son. Word had leaked out that Eddie O'Hara was an informant, and the news reached Al Capone, who was by that time serving time at Alcatraz. A team of gunmen was recruited from the Egan's Rats gang of St. Louis, and plans were set in motion to kill O'Hare.

It is thought that Frank Wilson's warnings made an impression on O'Hare. He was still enjoying considerable success in his professional life as the president of the Sportsman's Park racetrack in Stickney, developer of legal dog racing tracks, manager of the Chicago Cardinals football team, real estate investor and owner of an insurance company and two advertising agencies. In spite of his wealth and the respect that he earned as a business leader, he became a very paranoid man. Remembering Wilson's words, O'Hare began carrying a gun with him every day. On the day he was murdered, however, he never had a chance to draw it from its holster.

On November 8, 1939, O'Hare was driving from the dining room at the Illinois Athletic Club on Michigan Avenue to his office at the racetrack. He had no idea that his assassins were waiting for him at Twenty-second

The last photo of Eddie O'Hare, who was shot to death in his Lincoln Zephyr automobile on West Ogden Avenue. *Courtesy of the Library of Congress.*

Street and Ogden Avenue. As O'Hare drove past the intersection, a car pulled out and followed close behind him. Moments later, the car pulled alongside him as he approached 2601 West Ogden. O'Hare clumsily tried to pull out his gun, but it was too late. Two men fired shotguns from the other car, and Eddie was hit in the face and head. The new

Lincoln Zephyr automobile that he was driving swerved sharply, jumped the curb, rattled over the streetcar tracks and smashed into a trolley pole in the center lane. The second car roared away, and O'Hare's killers were never found.

Inside the wrecked car, the police found O'Hare's handgun, and the items in his pockets included a rosary, a crucifix, a religious medallion, a love note to a girlfriend that he had written in Italian and a poem that he had apparently clipped from a magazine. "Margy, Oh, Margy," the note read, "*Quanto tempo io penso per te. Fammi passer una notte insieme con te.*" ("How often I think of you. Let me spend the night with you.") The poem read:

> *The clock of life is wound but once*
> *And no man has the power*
> *To tell just when the hands will stop*
> *At late or early hour.*
> *Now is the only time you own.*
> *Live, love, toil with a will.*
> *Place no faith in time.*
> *For the clock may soon be still.*

It could have easily served as an epitaph for Eddie O'Hare.

The End of Innocence
in Chicago

One of the most shocking and terrifying crimes in the history of Chicago took place in October 1955, when the bodies of three boys were discovered in a virtually crime-free neighborhood on the West Side of the city. The Schuessler-Peterson murders stunned the city, and the horrific events—which would remain unsolved for forty years—changed the face of Chicago forever. Many called it the true end of innocence for a city that could hardly fathom the idea of brutal crimes being carried out against children.

Events began on a cool Sunday afternoon in the fall of 1955, when three boys from the West Side of Chicago headed downtown to catch a matinee performance of a Walt Disney nature film called *The African Lion* at the Loop Theatre. It was a trip with the most innocent of motives, and one made with the consent of the boys' parents. In those days, parents thought little of their responsible children going off on excursions by themselves. The boys had always proven dependable in the past, and this time would have been no exception if tragedy had not occurred. Bobby Peterson's mother had chosen the film for her son and his two friends, Anton and John Schuessler, and had sent them on their way with four dollars in loose change between them. It should have been plenty of money to keep them occupied for an afternoon and safely get them back home again.

What happened when the movie ended, however, still remains a mystery.

The matinee ended that afternoon, but for some reason, at about six o'clock that evening, the boys were reported in the lobby of the Garland

Newspaper photos of the boys that ran after their bodies were discovered. *From left to right*: Bobby Peterson, John Schuessler and John's brother, Anton. *Courtesy of the* Charleston Daily Mail.

Building at 111 North Wabash. There was no explanation for what they might have been doing there, other than that Bobby's eye doctor had an office in the building. It seems unlikely that he would have been visiting the optometrist on a Sunday afternoon, but his signature did appear on the lobby registry for that day, so he was obviously there. The Garland had a reputation in those days for being a hangout for homosexual prostitutes and hustlers, but if that had anything to do with the boys being there, no one knows.

Some have surmised that the trio only stopped long enough to use the restroom, since Bobby knew there was one available on the ninth floor, where his optometrist's office was located. They may have hurried up to the ninth floor and then headed right back out again. They were only believed to have been at the Garland for less than five minutes.

About 7:45 p.m., the three entered the Monte Cristo Bowling Alley at 3226 West Montrose Avenue. The bowling alley was a neighborhood eating place, and the proprietor later recalled to the police that he saw the boys and that a "fifty-ish-looking" man was showing an "abnormal interest" in several younger boys who were bowling. He was unable to say if this man had contact with the trio. The three left the bowling alley and walked down

Montrose to another bowling alley but were turned away because a league had taken over all of the available lanes for the evening.

Out of money, but for some reason still not headed toward home, the boys hitched a ride at the intersection of Lawrence and Milwaukee Avenue. It was now 9:05 p.m., and their parents were beginning to get worried. They had reason to be, for the boys were never seen alive again.

Two days later, their three naked and bound bodies were discovered in a shallow ditch near a parking lot about one hundred feet east of the Des Plaines River. A salesman, who had stopped to eat his lunch at the Robinson Woods Indian Burial Grounds nearby, spotted them and called the police. Coroner Walter McCarron stated that the cause of death was "asphyxiation by suffocation." The three boys had been dead about thirty-six hours when they were discovered. McCarron also declared that the killing had been a "sex crime" and the work of a "madman" or a "teen gang." It was, he stated, "the most horrible sex crime in years."

Bobby Peterson had been struck repeatedly and strangled with a rope or a necktie. Newspaper reports said that he had been slashed across the head fourteen times with a knife or an axe. The Schuessler brothers, it appeared, had been strangled by hand and had been hit on their faces with what appeared to be the flat side of a knife. The killer had used adhesive tape to cover the eyes of all three victims. They had then been dragged or thrown from a vehicle. Their clothing was never found.

The city of Chicago was thrown into a panic. Police officials reported that they had never seen such a horrible crime. The fears of parents all over the city were summed up by the shaken Anton Schuessler Sr., who said, "When you get to the point that children cannot go to the movies in the afternoon and get home safely, something is wrong with this country."

Police officers combed the area, conducting door-to-door searches and neighborhood interrogations. Search teams combed Robinson Woods, looking for clues or items of clothing. The killer (or killers) had gone to great lengths to get rid of any signs of fingerprints or other traces of evidence. More than one hundred officers, joined by fifty soldiers from the nearby army antiaircraft base, gathered near Robinson Woods at daybreak and walked in lines spaced four or five feet apart, looking for anything out of place. Divers were sent into the depths of the Des Plaines River for clues, but nothing was found.

By this time, various city and suburban police departments had descended on the scene, running into one another and further hampering the search for clues. There was little or no cooperation between the separate agencies,

The Schuessler-Peterson crime scene at Robinson Woods. Within hours of the bodies being discovered, any possible clues were destroyed by well-intentioned police officers and volunteers. *Courtesy of the* Charleston Daily Mail.

and if anything had been discovered, it would have most likely been lost in the confusion.

Away from the scene, patrolmen and detectives conducted a huge roundup of known sex deviates, especially those known to work in, or frequent, bowling alleys. They were convinced that this is where the boys had come into contact with the killer or killers. Most of the investigators were convinced that a gang of some sort had been at work, finding it hard to believe that all three boys could have been killed otherwise. Coroner McCarron extended the possibility that they "fell into the hands of a group of older boys and were manhandled."

While the city remained in stunned shock, the investigation stumbled along under the leadership of Cook County sheriff Joseph D. Lohman, who searched in desperation for some answers in the case. He even offered $2,500 from his personal bank account for information leading to an arrest. Lohman was admittedly in over his head, and he found himself under unwanted scrutiny by the newspapers, which sensationalized the murders, and the general public, which was collectively terrified.

Lohman was quoted in the *Chicago Tribune* as stating, "Chances are, the attackers were persons close to the boys' own age, who might have known them." He also pointed to indications that the victims had been held captive before they were killed and may have been slain because something had "gone wrong" and the captors wanted to make sure they were not identified. He said that Bobby, who took the worst beating, might have been killed first.

Not to leave out any possible theories, Lohman also went the other way and later surmised that the slayer was a "burly madman" or that two men had committed the crime. He noted that the "bodies had been thrown like bags of potatoes" and that this "would suggest that at least two persons or one very powerful person did it."

The first suspect picked up in the case was an unemployed schoolteacher, who was brought in for questioning early in the morning. He lived five blocks from the Schuessler home and had been named in an anonymous telephone call to the police. He was questioned vigorously, but after offering to take a lie detector test, he was released. He would not be the last "person of interest" to be questioned in the case, but time after time, men were interrogated and then let go.

While investigators were coming up empty, newspaper reporters hounded the grief-stricken parents of the three boys. The press descended on their neighborhood of modest bungalow homes, a place where crime of any kind was rare. It was almost impossible for them to fathom what

The grieving parents of two of the boys, John and Anton Schuessler. *Courtesy of the* Charleston Daily Mail.

had occurred. Murder was something that happened in the newspapers, not in their own neighborhood.

Mrs. Schuessler, described in the papers as a "frail 37-year-old woman," rocked back and forth on her living room couch on the day the bodies were found, surrounded by friends and neighbors. Reporters pushed into the room, looking for comments, but she only murmured things like "My life, my arms…my legs…now gone." Once she shrieked, "I want my boys! I want my—" before collapsing into hysterics.

Mr. Schuessler rushed into the room and fell to his knees in front of the couch where his wife was sitting. He shuddered with pain and apparent agony. "Mother, mother," he cried. "What kind of land do we live in?" He buried his face in her lap and sobbed.

The investigation continued with no results as the last days of Bobby Peterson and Anton and John Schuessler ended on a grim note. An honor guard of Boy Scouts carried the coffins of the three boys from the St. Tarcissus Roman Catholic Church to a hearse that would take them to St. Joseph Cemetery. The church was filled to capacity with an estimated twelve hundred mourners, and even more people joined the families at the graveside service, reaching crowds of over three thousand people. Reverend Raymond G. Carey told the gathering that "God has permitted sin, evil and suffering because He knows that He can bring good from the suffering."

No one present could see much in the way of good from the deaths of three innocent young boys, however. This marked the end of innocence in Chicago. It was now apparent to all that America had changed for the worse.

Years passed. Because there is no statute of limitations for murder, the case remained officially open, but there seemed to be little chance that it would ever be solved. The Schuessler-Peterson murders became a cautionary tale in Chicagoland, painting a bloody picture of what happened when children talked to strangers.

Four decades later, and after the principals in the case had long since passed away, a bizarre turn of events occurred that would finally offer closure for the cold case. In the mid-1990s, a government informant named William "Red" Wemette accused a man named Kenneth Hansen of the Schuessler-Peterson murders during a police investigation into the 1977 disappearance of candy heiress Helen Vorhees Brach.

In 1955, Hansen, then twenty-two years old, worked as a stable hand for Silas Jayne, a millionaire from Kane County. Jayne himself was wild and reckless and had been suspected of many violent and devious dealings during his rise to power in the horse-breeding world. He went to prison in

1973 for the murder of his half brother, George, and died of leukemia in 1987, escaping punishment for many of the crimes that were later laid at his doorstep.

Hansen had certainly committed plenty of crimes himself. The homosexual hustler later admitted to molesting as many as one thousand young boys, and investigators were easily able to build a case against him, thanks to the missing pieces filled in by Wemette. The renewed investigation resulted in his arrest in August 1994.

Cook County prosecutors showed jurors how Hansen had lured the Schuessler brothers and Bobby Peterson into his car under false pretenses near the intersection of Lawrence and Milwaukee Avenues. They retraced the path of the killer to Silas Jayne's Idle Hour Stables in the 8600 block of Higgins Road. Hansen's story was that he wanted to show the boys some prize horses that were being kept there. According to the testimony of several men Hansen had bragged to, he had molested and then killed Alton, John and Bobby one by one.

The boys were killed in the tack room when they tried to fight Hansen. Afterward, he tied up the bodies and then he and his brother (allegedly) dumped them at Robinson Woods. In the spring of 1956, the Idle Hours Stables burned to the ground. The week before the fire, the Cook County coroner had announced to the press that he planned to exhume the bodies of the three boys in a search for trace evidence. Silas Jayne, after seeing the newspaper report, became convinced that remnants of his stables might remain on the boys. Police detectives had previously visited the stable when they were following up on reports of boys' screams coming from the building at night. Jayne worried that they might connect the stables with Hansen's crime, which would have dire results for his own criminal operations. Out of fear, he torched the building to obliterate all of the evidence. The detectives never connected the arson to the murders, and Hansen managed to stay off the suspect list for nearly forty years.

When the case came to trial in 1995, four decades of silence were broken. Many of Hansen's other victims came forward, recalling promises of jobs made to young men in return for sexual favors. He had kept them silent with threats that included warnings that they might end up "like the Peterson boy." Even without evidence and eyewitnesses to corroborate the prosecution's allegations against him, a Cook County jury convicted Kenneth Hansen of the murders in September 1995. They deliberated for less than two hours, and Hansen was sentenced to two hundred to three hundred years in prison.

But the case was not yet over. In May 2000, the Illinois Appellate Court overturned Hansen's conviction. Two of the three justices found that the judge in the case erred when he allowed evidence to be submitted that showed that Hansen regularly picked up hitchhikers and sexually abused them. Despite what some saw as a close call, Hansen was almost routinely convicted again, and once more, he received the two-hundred- to three-hundred-year sentence. The Illinois Appellate Court affirmed the conviction in 2004, and this time, it appeared that Hansen would die behind bars.

Bobby, John and Anton could finally rest in peace.

THE BLOODY END OF ROGER "THE TERRIBLE" TOUHY

If there was any mobster from the Prohibition era who didn't deserve to die a bloody and violent death, it was Roger "the Terrible" Touhy. He was shot to death on the front porch of his sister's house just twenty-three days after he was paroled from the penitentiary in Joliet, where he had been serving time for a crime that he didn't commit.

Touhy never claimed to be an innocent man, but he did resent the fact that he ended up in prison for something he didn't do. He admitted that he had committed plenty of crimes over the years, however.

During Prohibition, Touhy was the head of a bootlegging gang whose territory included the West Side of Chicago and the suburbs of Morton Grove and Niles Center (now Skokie). Touhy and his four brothers—Tommy, James, John and Joe—worked closely together, kept to themselves and never purposely caused problems for the Capone organization. Their only goal was to make money with illegal beer, union collections and a handful of extortion rackets. They kept a respectful distance from other criminal gangs and expected them to keep their distance from the Touhys. Unfortunately, things didn't always work out that way.

Roger Touhy grew up at Ogden Avenue and Roosevelt Road on the city's West Side. His father, James, was an Irish immigrant who became a police officer. He and his wife had six sons and one daughter, all of whom were left in James's care after his wife perished in a fire. Roger was a very young boy when his mother died, and he had no memories of her. His father did the best he could to raise his spirited sons, but with little supervision, they fell in with a bad lot. Only one of the boys, Eddie, stayed out of trouble and became a bartender.

Like his brother, Roger also stayed away from crime, although only for a while. He dropped out of school after the eighth grade and worked at various times as a telegrapher, an oil field worker and a union organizer. He enlisted in the U.S. Navy during World War I. After the war, Roger married Clara Morgan in 1923. He became a cab driver and then an automobile salesman. He did very well selling cars, but his brother Tommy convinced him to form a trucking company with him in Des Plaines.

With the onset of Prohibition, Touhy and his brother began distributing illegal beer and liquor in the western suburbs. Touhy's other brothers got involved with the business, and Roger also partnered with Matt Kolb, who was already supplying the Capone Outfit with one-third of its beer, as well as running highly profitable gambling and protection rackets on the West Side. Together, Touhy and Kolb established a brewery and began producing high-quality beer. They were soon selling more than one thousand barrels a week.

In 1926, Touhy expanded his gambling operations and installed slot machines in taverns throughout the northwest suburbs. His slot machine operations alone grossed over $1 million over the course of the first year.

By the late 1920s, the Capone organization was ordering hundreds of barrels of beer each week from Roger Touhy. Envious of the operations that Touhy had on the northwest side, and now reluctant to keep paying for his beer, Capone decided that he wanted to take over Touhy's operation. He sent Jack "Machine Gun" McGurn and Louis "Little New York" Campagna to Touhy's headquarters to make him an offer that he couldn't refuse. But Touhy refused their demands. He was happy to continue doing business with Capone, but he would not turn over his operations to him.

Capone continued to send representatives to Touhy, and he also began to test Touhy's strength. Sporadic gun battles between Touhy's and Capone's men occurred in rural Cook County over the next several years. When Touhy won the support of Chicago mayor Anton Cermak, the increasingly frequent attempted hits began occurring inside the city limits as well. It was during this time that Touhy gained his nickname, "the Terrible."

The beer wars with Capone led to bloodshed and death for the Touhys. Roger's brother, John, was gunned down in 1927 while running beer in Niles. Another brother, Joseph, was gunned down two years later.

In 1931, two more gunmen from the Capone organization, Frank Rio and Willie Heeney, went to threaten Touhy. At this time, Touhy had few gunmen in his employ, and he knew that Capone was trying to take advantage of this. Taking a chance, Touhy approached the local police and asked them for their support. He explained to them that he only wanted to sell liquor, but if Capone took over his operation, the police could count on lawlessness, gambling and prostitution following close behind. Worried local leaders agreed to help. When Rio and Heeney met with Touhy, several dozen off-duty police officers and local farmers lounged around the building with guns. The show of force unnerved Capone's men, and they reported back to the boss that Touhy's gang had over one hundred gunmen.

Later that summer, the Capone gang made another move against Touhy by going after his partner, Matt Kolb. Very early in the morning after the day that Capone was convicted on tax evasion charges, two well-dressed men walked into Kolb's Club Morton roadhouse in Morton Grove and asked to speak to the owner. Kolb came out, shook hands with the men and spoke with them for a few minutes. Then, in a move that was reminiscent of the assassination of Dion O'Banion, one of the men grabbed hold of Kolb while his partner pulled out a gun and shot Kolb six times in the head. On the way out, the gunman walked back to the fallen man and shot him again, just to make sure that he was dead.

The war between the Outfit and the Touhy organization continued, but since violence had failed to bring down Touhy, the Outfit decided that it would be easier to get rid of its rival using the law.

In 1933, Touhy was arrested for the kidnapping of William A. Hamm, the brewery heir. The kidnapping had actually been carried out by the Barker-Karpis gang, and there was nothing but hearsay and an anonymous tip that linked Touhy to the crime. (Hamm was released by the Barkers and Alvin Karpis four days after the payment of a $100,000 ransom.) Nevertheless, Touhy and three others were indicted on kidnapping charges on August 12, 1933. They were found not guilty on November 28.

While awaiting release after the Hamm kidnapping trial, Touhy was arrested again on December 4, 1933—this time for the kidnapping of John "Jake the Barber" Factor, half brother of cosmetics mogul Max Factor.

The Factor kidnapping was a carefully organized frame-up, orchestrated by the Capone mob, Dan Gilbert and Tom Courtney, a ruthless district attorney. Gilbert, who had numerous connections to organized crime, and Courtney controlled the Cook County courts in the mid-1930s, and their clout reached into the court system, the police department and city hall.

Bootlegger Roger Touhy in court for the kidnapping of beer heir William A. Hamm. Touhy is in the center of the front row. *Courtesy of Corbis.*

Factor and the Capone Outfit had arranged to fake the kidnapping and produce evidence that made it look as though Touhy was involved. The plan was a risky one. Factor himself was a known criminal and was on the run from British authorities, who were after him on mail fraud charges. Touhy had already been implicated in the Hamm kidnapping and was under police watch at the time of the Factor kidnapping. Nevertheless, on July 1, 1933, Factor was abducted outside of the Dells roadhouse in Morton Grove. Factor's wife paid a $75,000 ransom twelve days later, and her husband was "released." It was later discovered that Factor spent the entire time hiding out in a cabin in Wauconda, Illinois.

Roger Touhy and three of his men went on trial for the John Factor kidnapping on January 15, 1934. Factor himself said that he recognized Roger Touhy's voice among the kidnappers and was able to identify him during a lineup. Most of the other witnesses were not as compelling. Most of them proved to be completely unreliable on the witness stand, and later evidence showed that a number of prosecution witnesses perjured themselves in the attempt to convict Touhy. One juror refused to report for duty midway through the trial, and another juror admitted that he had lied about his knowledge of the case as the jury was being seated. A mistrial was declared on February 2, 1934.

A second trial began on February 13. Once more, prosecution witnesses perjured themselves on the stand and the jury convicted Touhy and his three associates on February 22. Touhy was sentenced to ninety-nine years at the Stateville Penitentiary in Joliet.

Touhy immediately filed an appeal, and over the course of the next eight years, he spent most of his bootlegging fortune on legal fees. But he was fighting an uphill battle. With Gilbert and Courtney still influencing the Cook County courts, he knew that he was not going to get a fair break. So on October 9, 1942, he took matters into his own hands and broke out of Stateville with six other men. One month later, Touhy was discovered living in a Chicago boardinghouse. He surrendered peacefully and went back to prison with 199 years tacked on for the prison break.

In 1944, the 20th Century Fox studio released a highly fictionalized film based on Touhy's life called *Roger Touhy, Gangster*. Touhy successfully sued the studio for defamation of character, and he received a $10,000 award six years later. Fox agreed not to distribute the film domestically but could still show it overseas.

Touhy continued his legal battles from behind bars, and on August 9, 1954, a federal district court ruled that he should be released. The court found that the Factor kidnapping had been a hoax and that Touhy's conviction had been obtained with false testimony. The court also ruled that the state's lead investigator and the state's attorney had known of the perjured testimony but kept that information from the defense. Unfortunately, Touhy was back behind bars in less than two days. A federal court of appeals ruled that the district court lacked jurisdiction to hear the case because Touhy had not yet exhausted his state appeals. Roger Touhy still couldn't get a fair break.

Finally, in 1959, Illinois governor William G. Stratton commuted Touhy's sentence and paved the way for his parole on November 19. Touhy left Stateville on November 24, after spending twenty-five years and nine months in prison for a crime he didn't commit.

After his release, Touhy quietly sought refuge at a bungalow that was owned by his sister, Ethel Alesia, at 125 North Lotus Avenue on Chicago's West Side. "The freedom is wonderful," he told Ray Brennan, a reporter for the *Chicago Sun-Times* and the man who was working with Touhy to write his autobiography. The book was mostly meant to be an account

Touhy after his release from prison in 1959. He served twenty-five years and nine months for a crime that he didn't commit.

of the Factor kidnapping that had landed him behind bars. In the book, Touhy never claimed to be an angel but stated that the kidnapping was a hoax that had been perpetrated by people on both sides of the law. Aside from the Outfit, Touhy pointed fingers at Dan Gilbert, John Factor and state's attorney Tom Courtney. It was plain from his writings that the people with the most to gain from his downfall were members of the former Capone organization.

The Bloody End of Roger "the Terrible" Touhy

Few of the Outfit members remained by the time Touhy got out of prison. Capone and Frank Nitti had both died years before. Only mob fixer Murray "the Camel" Humphreys had a lot to lose if Touhy continued with his crusade. Humphreys had settled into relative obscurity over the years. He was still running several mob operations, but things were quiet for him, and he wanted to keep them that way. He and Touhy had clashed many times during union troubles in years past.

Perfectly aware of his position as a prison parolee, Touhy feared someone slipping a phony parole rap on him, so he hired a bodyguard to watch his back. The man he hired was Walter Miller, a former police investigator who had discovered the Wauconda cabin where Factor had hidden out during his phony abduction and tried to set the record straight. He had been ordered not to talk about it, or risk the consequences, and this made Touhy believe that Miller was the right man to keep him safe.

The blood-soaked steps at Ethel's house at 125 North Lotus Avenue on the West Side. Touhy's murder was committed by someone who wanted him to keep quiet about the kidnapping hoax that had landed him in Stateville Penitentiary.

John "Jake the Barber" Factor reading a newspaper article about Touhy's murder. *Courtesy of Corbis.*

In spite of this, Touhy kept his forays around town to a minimum, and his sister insisted that he return home at least a half hour before his 11:00 p.m. curfew, just in case. Touhy was not in fear for his life—he just didn't want to go back to prison.

On December 16, 1959, Touhy and Miller spent the evening in the Loop with writer Ray Brennan. The writer left about 9:30 p.m., and Touhy and Miller returned to Ethel's bungalow about 10:15 p.m. They climbed out of the car and went up the seven concrete steps from the walk to the open porch at the front of the brick home. As the pair made it to the top step, two men appeared from the shadows and unloaded five shotgun blasts at them. Miller managed to fire off three shots at the fleeing men before he collapsed. Touhy fell to the porch, a fist-sized wound in his upper left leg and dozens of pellet-sized wounds all over his body. He was bleeding badly, and by the time the ambulance arrived, blood had dripped down all seven steps to the concrete sidewalk below. Remarkably, Touhy remained conscious. "I'll be all right, I'm okay," he assured police officers and ambulance attendants. Less than an hour later, Roger Touhy was dead.

At the time Touhy was murdered, John Factor was dining in a nearby North Side restaurant. When asked, Factor expressed sympathy for Walter Miller's plight (the bodyguard survived the shooting), but about Touhy, he simply said, "It's not my way of life. I feel very badly. It's too bad for any human being to be cut down like that."

Factor had filed a $3 million libel suit against Touhy in the event that he released his book. Because of his murder, the final chapter of the book, which Touhy and Brennan called "The Stolen Years," was never written. Factor's lawsuit against Brennan was later settled out of court. Factor received a pardon in 1962 from President John F. Kennedy for the charges that would have sent him back to Britain. He was a generous contributor to Kennedy's 1960 campaign and a friend of the Las Vegas Rat Pack. Factor reportedly ran the Stardust Casino in Las Vegas for the mob in later years.

Roger Touhy's killers were never found, but the mob was always the leading suspect. Investigators pointed out that while Touhy in prison was just another convict, outside prison walls, he was bad publicity for the Outfit. A *Chicago Tribune* press editorial stated:

> *In a world where there are few roses, Roger Touhy did not pretend to be one, but his finish emphasizes that even a man who was not so good may be the victim of men who are worse.*

JOHN WAYNE GACY

THE CLOWN WHO KILLED

To everyone who met him, John Wayne Gacy seemed a likable and affable man. He was widely respected in the community, charming and easy to get along with. He was a good Catholic and sharp businessman who, when not running his construction company, was active in the Jaycees and with community volunteer groups. When he was a Democratic Party precinct captain, he had his photo taken with then first lady Rosalynn Carter. He also spent much of his free time hosting elaborate street parties for his friends and neighbors and entertaining children as "Pogo the Clown." He was a generous, hardworking, friendly, devoted family man, everyone knew that—but that was the side of John Wayne Gacy that he allowed people to see.

Underneath the smiling mask of the clown was the face of a depraved madman.

John Wayne Gacy was born on March 17, 1942, at Edgewater Hospital in Chicago, the second of three children. The Gacy children were raised in a Catholic home, and all three attended Catholic schools on the North Side. Growing up, Gacy was a quiet boy who worked odd jobs, like newspaper routes and bagging groceries, for spending money and busied himself with Boy Scout activities. He was never a particularly popular boy, but he was well liked by his teachers, co-workers and friends from school and the Boy Scouts. He seemed to have a normal childhood, except for his relationship with his father and a series of health problems.

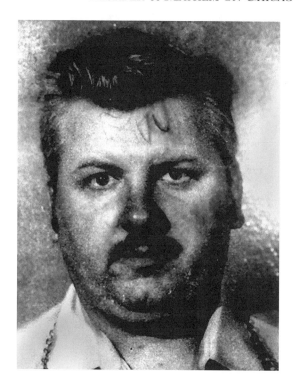

Depraved serial killer John Wayne Gacy. On the surface, he was a likable man and a good neighbor, but a madman lurked under his mask of respectability. *Courtesy of the Library of Congress.*

When Gacy was eleven, he was playing on a swing set and was hit in the head with one of the swings. The accident caused a blood clot in his brain that was not discovered until he was sixteen. Between the time of the accident and the diagnosis, Gacy suffered from blackouts caused by the clot. These were eventually treated with medication. At seventeen, he was also diagnosed with a heart ailment that led to his hospitalization several times during his life.

In his late teens, he began to experience problems with his father, although his relationship with his mother and sisters remained strong. His father was an alcoholic who physically abused his wife and berated his children. He was an unpleasant individual, but Gacy loved his father and constantly worked to gain his attention and approval. Gacy Sr. died before his son could ever get close to him.

Gacy's family problems had an effect on his schoolwork, and after attending four high schools during his senior year and never graduating, he dropped out and left home for Las Vegas. He worked part time as a janitor in a funeral home and saved his money to buy a ticket back to

Chicago. Lonely and depressed, he spent three months trying to get the money together. His mother and sisters were thrilled to see him when he came home.

After his return, Gacy enrolled in business college and eventually graduated. While in school, he gained a real talent for salesmanship, and he put these talents to work in a job with the Nunn-Bush Shoe Company. He excelled as a management trainee, and he was soon transferred to a men's clothing outlet in Springfield, Illinois.

While living in Springfield, Gacy became involved in several organizations that served the community, including the Jaycees, to which Gacy devoted most of his efforts. He was eventually voted vice-president of the local chapter and named Man of the Year. Those who knew Gacy considered him to be ambitious and someone who was working hard to make a name for himself in the community. He was an overachiever who worked so diligently that he had to be hospitalized for nervous exhaustion on one occasion.

In September 1964, Gacy met and married a co-worker named Marlynn Myers, whose parents owned a number of Kentucky Fried Chicken restaurants in Iowa. Gacy's new father-in-law offered him a position with the company, and soon the newlyweds moved to Iowa.

Gacy began learning the restaurant business from the ground up, working twelve to fourteen hours each day. He was enthusiastic and eager to learn and hoped to take over the franchises one day. When not working, he was active with the Waterloo, Iowa Jaycees. He worked tirelessly performing volunteer work, and he made many friends. Marlynn gave birth to a son shortly after the couple moved to Iowa, and not long after, they added a daughter to the happy family. They seemed to have the picture-perfect life, but trouble was already starting.

Rumors were starting to spread around town, and among Jaycees members, about Gacy's sexual preferences. No one could help but notice that young boys always seemed to be in his presence. Stories spread that he had made passes at some of the young men who worked in the restaurants, but those close to him refused to believe it—until the rumors became hard fact. In May 1968, a grand jury in Black Hawk County indicted Gacy for committing an act of sodomy with a teenage boy named Mark Miller. The boy told the courts that Gacy had tricked him into being tied up while visiting Gacy's home and then had violently raped him. Gacy denied the charges but did say that Miller willingly had sex with him in order to earn extra money.

Four months later, more charges were filed against Gacy. This time, he was charged with hiring an eighteen-year-old boy named Dwight Andersson to beat up Mark Miller. Andersson lured Miller to his car and then drove him to a wooded area, where he sprayed mace in his eyes and began to beat him. Miller fought back, breaking Andersson's nose, and managed to run away. He called the police, and Andersson was picked up and taken into police custody. He informed the officer that Gacy had hired him to attack the other boy.

Soon after, Gacy entered a guilty plea on the earlier sodomy charge. He received a ten-year sentence at the Iowa State Reformatory, the maximum time for the offense, and entered prison for the first time at the age of twenty-six. Shortly after he went to jail, his wife divorced him on the grounds that he had violated their wedding vows.

Gacy was a model prisoner and was paroled after only eighteen months. In June 1970, he made his way back to Chicago. He moved in with his mother and obtained work as a chef in a city restaurant.

Gacy lived with his mother for four months and then decided to move out on his own. She helped him obtain a new house at 8213 West Summerdale Avenue in the Norwood Park Township on Chicago's West Side. Gacy owned one-half of the house, and his mother and sisters owned the other. The new, two-bedroom ranch house was located in a clean, quiet neighborhood, and Gacy quickly went about making friends with his neighbors, Edward and Lillie Grexa. Within seven months of moving in next door, Gacy was spending Christmas with the Grexas. They became close friends and often gathered for drinks and card games.

In June 1972, Gacy married Carole Hoff, a newly divorced mother of two girls. Gacy romanced her when she was most vulnerable, and she fell for his charm and generosity. She knew about his time in prison but believed that he had changed his life for the better. Carole and her daughters soon settled into Gacy's home and forged a close relationship with the Grexas. The older couple was often invited over to the Gacys' place for elaborate parties and cookouts. However, they were bothered by the horrible stench that sometimes wafted throughout the house. Lillie Grexa was convinced that an animal had died beneath the floorboards of the place, and she urged Gacy to do something about it. He blamed the odor on a moisture buildup in the crawl space under the house.

In 1974, Gacy started a contracting business called Painting, Decorating and Maintenance, or PDM Contractors, Inc. He hired a number of teenage boys to work for him and explained to friends that hiring young men would keep his payroll costs low. In truth, Gacy's secrets were starting to catch up with him, and they were starting to become very apparent to those who knew him, especially his wife.

By 1975, Carole and Gacy had drifted apart. Their sex life had ended, and Gacy's moods became more and more unpredictable, ranging from jovial to uncontrollable rage that would have him throwing furniture. He had become an insomniac, and his lack of sleep seemed to make his mood swings even worse. And if his personality changes were not enough, his choice of reading material worried her even more. Carole started to find magazines filled with naked men and boys around the house, and when confronted, Gacy casually admitted they were his. He even confessed that he preferred young men to women. Naturally, this was the last straw for Carole, and she soon filed for divorce. It became final on March 2, 1976.

Gacy dismissed his marital problems and refused to let them hamper his need for recognition and success. To most people, Gacy was still the outgoing and hardworking man that he always had been, and he always came up with creative ways to get himself noticed. It was not long before he gained the attention of Robert F. Matwick, the Democratic township committeeman for Norwood Park. As a free service to the committeeman, Gacy volunteered himself and his employees to clean up and repair the Democratic Party headquarters. Unaware of the contractor's past and impressed by his sense of duty and dedication to the community, Matwick nominated Gacy to the streetlighting commission. In 1975, Gacy became the secretary treasurer, but his political career was short-lived. No matter how well he thought he was hiding it, rumors again began to circulate about Gacy's interest in young boys.

One of the rumors stemmed from an incident that took place during the time Gacy was working on the Democratic headquarters. One of the teenagers who worked on the project was sixteen-year-old Tony Antonucci. According to the boy, Gacy made sexual advances toward him but backed off when Antonucci threatened to hit him with a chair. Gacy recovered his composure and made a joke out of it. He tried to convince Tony that he was only kidding and left him alone for the next month.

Several weeks later, Gacy again approached Antonucci while the boy was visiting Gacy's home. He tricked the young man into a pair of handcuffs and then tried to undress him. Antonucci had made sure that he was loosely cuffed, and when he slipped free, he wrestled Gacy to the ground and cuffed the older man instead. He eventually let him go when Gacy promised not to bother him again. That was the last time Gacy ever made advances toward

Antonucci, and the boy remained working for the contracting company for almost a year after the incident. Tony Antonucci never realized how lucky he was that day.

Others would not fare so well.

Johnny Butkovich, age seventeen, began doing remodeling work for Gacy's company in an effort to raise money for his racing car. He enjoyed the position, it paid well and he maintained a good working relationship with Gacy, until one pay period when Gacy refused to pay Johnny for two weeks of work. Angered that Gacy had withheld his pay, Johnny went over to his employer's house with two friends to collect what was rightfully his. When confronted, Gacy refused to pay, and a loud argument erupted. Finally, Johnny realized that there was little he could do, and he and his friends left. He dropped off his friends at home and drove away—never to be seen again.

Michael Bonnin, age seventeen, enjoyed working with his hands, especially doing carpentry and woodworking. He often had several different projects going at the same time. In June 1976, he had almost completed restoring an antique jukebox but never got the opportunity to finish the job. He was on his way to catch a train to meet his stepfather's brother when he vanished.

Billy Carroll, age sixteen, was a longtime troublemaker who had first been in trouble with the authorities at the age of nine. Two years later, he was caught with a gun. He spent most of his life on the streets of Chicago, making money by arranging meetings between teenage boys and adult men for a commission. Although he came from a very different background than Michael Bonnin and Johnny Butkovich, all three had one thing in common—John Wayne Gacy. Like the others, Carroll disappeared suddenly. He left home on June 13, 1976, and was never seen alive again.

Gregory Godzik, age seventeen, started working for PDM Contractors in order to finance parts for his 1966 Pontiac. The work that he did for Gacy paid well and he liked it. On December 12, 1976, Gregory dropped his date at her house and drove toward home. The following day, the police found Gregory's Pontiac, but the boy was missing.

On January 20, 1977, John Szyc, age sixteen, vanished. He had driven off in his 1971 Plymouth Satellite and was never seen alive again. Szyc had not worked for PDM Contractors, but he was acquainted with Gregory Godzik, Johnny Butkovich and, fatally, John Wayne Gacy.

On September 15, 1977, Robert Gilroy, age eighteen, disappeared. Gilroy was an avid outdoorsman and was supposed to catch a bus to meet friends for horseback riding. When he never showed up, his father, a Chicago police sergeant, immediately began searching for the boy. A full-scale investigation was launched, but Robert was nowhere to be found.

Gacy's web of secrets began to unravel with the vanishing of a young boy named Robert Piest. The investigation into Piest's disappearance led to the discovery of not only the boy's body but also the bodies of Butkovich, Bonnin, Carroll, Szyc, Gilroy and twenty-seven other young men who suffered similar fates. These discoveries horrified Chicago and the nation as a whole.

Fifteen-year-old Robert Piest disappeared mysteriously just outside the doors of the pharmacy where he worked. His mother, who had come to pick him up after his shift, was waiting outside for him when he vanished. He had told her that he would be back in just a minute because he was going to talk to a contractor who had offered him a job. He never returned. She began to get worried, but as more time passed, her worry turned to terror. Finally, three hours after his disappearance, the Des Plaines police were notified. Lieutenant Joseph Kozenczak led the investigation.

The first lead to follow was the most obvious one, and officers quickly obtained the name of the contractor who had offered Robert the job. Kozenczak went straight to Gacy's home, and when Gacy came to the door, the officer told him about the missing boy. He also asked Gacy to accompany him to the police station for some questions. Gacy refused, explaining that there had been a recent death in his family and he had to attend to some telephone calls. He agreed to come down later. Several hours later, Gacy arrived at the station and gave a statement to the police. He said that he knew nothing about the disappearance and was allowed to leave with no further questioning.

Kozenczak decided to do a background check on Gacy. He was stunned when he discovered that he had done time for sodomy with a teenage boy. He quickly obtained a search warrant for Gacy's house, and on December 13, 1978, a legion of police officers entered the house on Summerdale Avenue. Gacy was not at home at the time.

The police were shocked by what they found. Some of the items discovered in the search included a box containing two driver's licenses and several rings; a box containing marijuana and amyl nitrate pills; a number of books with homosexual and child pornography themes; a pair of handcuffs; police badges; sexual devices; a hypodermic needle and small brown bottle; clothing that was too small for Gacy; nylon rope; and other items. The police also confiscated three automobiles that belonged to Gacy, including a 1978 Chevrolet truck with a snowplow attached and the name "PDM

Contractors" on the side, a van with "PDM Contractors" also painted on the side and a 1979 Oldsmobile Delta 88. In the trunk of the car were pieces of hair that were later matched to Robert Piest.

As the investigation continued, the police entered the crawl space under Gacy's home. They were discouraged by the rancid odor but believed it to be sewage. The earth in the crawl space had been sprinkled with lime but appeared to be untouched. They left the narrow space and returned to police headquarters to run tests on the evidence they had obtained.

Gacy was again called to headquarters and was told about the evidence that had been removed from his house. Enraged, he immediately contacted his attorney, who told him not to sign the Miranda waiver that was presented to him by detectives. The police had nothing to arrest him for and eventually had to release him after more questioning about the Piest disappearance. They placed him under twenty-four-hour surveillance, and over the next few days, his friends were called into the station and were also questioned. The detectives were unable to get any information from them that connected him to Robert Piest, and all of his friends insisted that Gacy simply was not capable of murder. Unable to gather other evidence, Gacy was finally charged with possession of marijuana.

Meanwhile, the police lab and investigators were coming up with critical evidence against Gacy from the items taken from his home. One of the rings found in Gacy's house belonged to another teenager who had disappeared about a year earlier, John Szyc. They also discovered that three former employees of Gacy's had also disappeared. Furthermore, a receipt for a roll of film that was found in Gacy's home had belonged to a co-worker of Robert Piest, and he had given it to Robert on the day of the boy's disappearance. With this new information, the investigators suddenly began to realize the enormity of the case that was starting to unfold.

Under questioning, Gacy tearfully confessed that he had killed someone in self-defense and, frightened, had buried the body under his garage. Detectives and crime lab technicians returned to Gacy's house again. They decided to search the crawl space under the house, as well as the garage. Minutes after starting to dig, they found the first corpse. Soon, a full-scale excavation was taking place.

On Friday, December 22, 1978, detectives confronted Gacy with the news that digging was being done under his house. With this, the monster finally broke down. He admitted to the police that he had killed at least thirty people and that most of their remains were buried beneath the house. The first murder took place in January 1972 and the second in

January 1974, about a year and a half after he was married. He explained that he lured his victims into being handcuffed and then sexually assaulted them. To muffle their screams, Gacy stuffed a sock, or their underwear, into their mouths. He would often kill them by placing a rope or board against their throats as he raped them. He also admitted to sometimes keeping the corpses under his bed or in his attic before burying them in the crawl space.

The police discovered two bodies during the first day of digging. One of these was John Butkovich, who was found under the garage, and the other body was in the crawl space. As the days passed, the body count grew higher. Some of the victims were found with their underwear still lodged in their throats, and others were buried so close together that investigators believed they had been killed, or at least buried, at the same time.

By December 28, the police had removed a total of twenty-seven bodies from Gacy's house. Another body had also been found weeks earlier, not in the crawl space but in the Des Plaines River. The naked corpse of Frank Wayne "Dale" Landingin was found in the water, but at the time, the police were not yet aware of Gacy and his crimes. It was not until Landingin's

The crawl space under Gacy's home was described as the most gruesome crime scene in Chicago's history. *Courtesy of the Library of Congress.*

driver's license was found in the house that Gacy was connected to the young man's murder.

The body of James Mazzara was also removed from the Des Plaines River. His underwear was found stuffed down his throat, linking him to the other victims. Gacy told the police that he had started disposing of bodies in the river because he was running out of room in his crawl space.

Much to the horror of the neighbors, the police were still excavating Gacy's property at the end of February. They had gutted the house but had found no more bodies in the crawl space. Bad winter weather kept them from resuming the search, but they believed there were still bodies to be found. As workmen began breaking up the concrete of Gacy's patio, another horrific discovery was made. They found the body of a man, still in good condition, preserved in the concrete. The following week, another body was found.

The thirty-first victim to be linked to Gacy was found in the Illinois River. Investigators were able to learn his identity thanks to a tattoo on his arm, which friends of the victim's father recognized while reading a newspaper article about the grim discovery. The victim's name was Timothy O'Rourke, and he was believed to have been acquainted with Gacy.

About the time that O'Rourke was discovered and pulled from the river, another body was found on Gacy's property, this time beneath his recreation room. It was the last body to be found on the property, and soon after, the house was reduced to rubble.

Although the death toll had now risen to thirty-two, the body of Robert Piest was still missing. His remains were discovered in the Illinois River in April 1979. The body had been lodged somewhere in the river, but strong winds had worked it loose and carried it to the locks at Dresden Dam, where it was finally discovered. An autopsy report showed that Robert had been strangled by paper towels being shoved down his throat.

Police investigators worked hard to identify Gacy's victims, using dental records and other clues, and eventually all but nine of the young men were identified. A mass burial was held for these unknown victims on June 8, 1981.

John Wayne Gacy's murder trial began on February 6, 1980, at the Cook County Criminal Courts Building in downtown Chicago. The defense argued that Gacy was insane and not in control of his actions, but the prosecution refuted this, stating that the murders, and subsequent disposal of the bodies, had been carried out in a deliberate manner. In their closing statements, both sides emotionally argued their cases, but the jury took only two hours of deliberation to come back with a guilty verdict. Gacy was convicted of the deaths of thirty-three young men and gained the notoriety of being convicted of more murders than anyone else in American history. He received the death penalty and was sent to the Menard Correctional Center to await execution. After years of appeals, he was put to death by lethal injection on May 9, 1994.

His death brought an end to one of the most terrifying periods in Chicago's criminal history. The mere mention of his name still manages to send a chill through the hearts of many, even after all these years.

BIBLIOGRAPHY

Adler, Jeffrey S. *First in Violence, Deepest in Dirt*. Cambridge, MA: Harvard University Press, 2006.

Asbury, Herbert. *Gem of the Prairie*. New York: Alfred A. Knopf, 1940.

Binder, John J. *The Chicago Outfit*. Chicago: Arcadia, 2003.

Chicago Historical Society

Chicago Public Library

Cowdery, Ray. *Capone's Chicago*. Lakeville, MN: Northstar Commemoratives, 1987.

Demaris, Ovid. *Captive City*. New York: Lyle Stuart, 1969.

Eghigian, Mars, Jr. *After Capone*. Nashville, TN: Cumberland House, 2006.

English, T.J. *Paddywhacked*. New York: HarperCollins, 2005.

Farr, Finis. *Chicago*. New Rochelle, NY: Arlington House, 1973.

Halper, Albert. *The Chicago Crime Book*. Cleveland, OH: World Publishing, 1967.

Helmer, William. *Public Enemies*. New York: Facts on File, 1998.

Helmer, William, and Arthur J. Bilek. *The St. Valentine's Day Massacre*. Nashville, TN: Cumberland House, 2004.

Helmer, William, and Rick Mattix. *The Complete Public Enemy Almanac*. Nashville, TN: Cumberland House, 2007.

Humble, Ronald D. *Frank Nitti*. Fort Lee, NJ: Barricade Books, 2007.

Johnson, Curt, with R. Craig Sautter. *Wicked City*. Highland Park, IL: December Press, 1994.

King, Jeffrey S. *Rise and Fall of the Dillinger Gang*. Nashville, TN: Cumberland House, 2005.

Kobler, John. *Capone*. New York: G.P. Putnam's Sons, 1971.

Lait, Jack, and Lee Mortimer. *Chicago Confidential*. New York: Crown Publishers, 1950.

Landesco, John. *Organized Crime in Chicago*. Chicago: University of Chicago Press, 1968.

Lesy, Michael. *Murder City*. New York: W.W. Norton & Co., 2007.

Lewis, Lloyd, and Henry Justin Smith. *Chicago*. New York: Harcourt, Brace & Co., 1929.

Lindberg, Richard. *Chicago by Gaslight*. Chicago: Chicago Academy Publishers, 1996.

———. *Return Again to the Scene of the Crime*. Nashville, TN: Cumberland House, 2001.

———. *Return to the Scene of the Crime*. Nashville, TN: Cumberland House, 1999.

Matera, Dary. *John Dillinger*. New York: Carroll & Graf, 2004.

Nash, Jay Robert. *Bloodletters and Bad Men*. New York: M. Evans and Company, Inc., 1995.

————. *Open Files*. New York: McGraw-Hill Book Co., 1983.

Nickel, Steven, and William J. Helmer. *Baby Face Nelson*. Nashville, TN: Cumberland House, 2002.

Poulsen, Ellen. *Don't Call Us Molls: Women of the John Dillinger Gang*. Little Neck, NY: Clinton Cook Publishing Corp, 2002.

Sifakis, Carl. *Encyclopedia of American Crime*. New York: Facts on File, 1982.

Taylor, Troy. *Bloody Chicago*. Decatur, IL: Whitechapel Press, 2006.

————. *Bloody Illinois*. Decatur, IL: Whitechapel Press, 2008.

————. *Dead Men Do Tell Tales*. Decatur, IL: Whitechapel Press, 2008.

Toland, John. *Dillinger Days*. New York: Da Capo Press, 1995.

Wright, Sewell Peaslee. *Chicago Murders*. New York: Duell, Sloan & Pierce, 1945.

NEWSPAPERS

Chicago American
Chicago Daily News
Chicago Herald-American
Chicago Herald & Examiner
Chicago Inter-Ocean
Chicago Sun-Times
Chicago Times
Chicago Tribune